GREAT PRESENTATION IDEAS

FROM SUCCESSFUL MANAGERS AND COMPANIES AROUND THE WORLD

Patrick Forsyth

D0109314

Marshall Cavendish
Business

First published in 2010 by Marshall Cavendish Business
An imprint of Marshall Cavendish International

PO Box 65829
London EC1P 1NY
United Kingdom
and
1 New Industrial Road, Singapore 536196
genrefsales@sg.marshallcavendish.com
www.marshallcavendish.com/genref

Other Marshall Cavendish offices: Marshall Cavendish International (Asia) Private Limited,
1 New Industrial Road, Singapore 536196 • Marshall Cavendish Corporation. 99 White Plains
Road, Tarrytown NY 10591-9001, USA • Marshall Cavendish International (Thailand) Co Ltd.
253 Asoke, 12th Flr, Sukhumvit 21 Road, Klongtoey Nua, Wattana, Bangkok 10110, Thailand •
Marshall Cavendish (Malaysia) Sdn Bhd, Times Subang, Lot 46, Subang Hi-Tech Industrial
Park, Batu Tiga, 40000 Shah Alam, Selangor Darul Ehsan, Malaysia

Marshall Cavendish is a trademark of Times Publishing Limited

A CIP record for this book is available from the British Library

ISBN 978-981-4276-91-7

Printed and bound in Great Britain by
TJ International Limited, Padstow, Cornwall

CONTENTS

Introduction   2

The ideas

Part 1 – Before You Start   **8**
1   The overall opportunity   9
2   Reading isn't speaking   11
3   A final rehearsal?   13
4   Your "presenting profile"   15
5   Setting objectives   18
6   An overall structure   21
7   Provide your own experience   23
8   You and your shadow   25
9   May the best man win   27
10 It is not just nerves   28
11 The right sort of crib   32
12 Time well spent   34
13 A bear of very little brain   36
14 Putting your message together   38
15 Speaker's notes: a suggested format   41
16 Maximizing the effectiveness of preparation   43
17 A guiding hand   45
18 I think, therefore I fail...   47
19 When the order of the day is mob handed   49

Part 2 – During The Presentation   **51**
20 First impressions last   52
21 Getting off to a good start   54
22 You want me to do what?   58
23 Speaking in tongues   60

24	The merits of a third column	62
25	Again and again and...	64
26	Wired for sound	66
27	Organizing the environment	68
28	Many, many, many...	71
29	Clear intentions	73
30	A handy glass	75
31	The audience	76
32	Every audience is different	79
33	The wonders of "B"	81
34	Taking questions	83
35	With a song in your...	85
36	A little sunshine	87
37	Hello to you, and hello to you too	88
38	Two important rules	90
39	Breaking the ice	92
40	Selecting the words you use	94
41	Sex... and other unmentionables	97
42	Some putting power	99
43	Take heed of the movies	101
44	Putting across the main content	103
45	That's funny, not	105
46	The sound of silence	107
47	Clear as a bell	109
48	The nature of numbers and number "blindness"	112
49	When people don't agree	115
50	Combating objections	117
51	A simple idea	119
52	Gaining acceptance	121
53	An idea that's what?	123
54	Engaging with the audience	125
55	I really must apologize...	127
56	Clear and memorable	129

57	On time	131
58	Some nifty footwork	134
59	Something unforeseen	137
60	Oops!	140
61	Are you standing comfortably?	142
62	Making a gesture	144
63	Using your voice	146
64	It's all in the breathing	148
65	Can you hear me at the back?	151
66	Ready, steady, go	153
67	The eyes have it	154
68	Pointing the way	157
69	Here's a funny thing	160
70	To, fro and back again	163
71	And finally, finally, finally...	165
72	A final flourish	167
73	The last word	169
74	No thanks	171

Part 3 – After The Presentation — **173**

75	Anyone have anything to say?	174
76	After the sigh of relief	176
77	Getting into the habit	178

Part 4 – Using Visual Aids — **180**

78	First up	181
79	The blind leading the blind	183
80	Worth a thousand words	185
81	Anything and everything	188
82	Beware gremlins	190
83	Can you see from the back?	192
84	Not on screen	194
85	Write tight	196

86 Bite-sized and manageable   198
87 A gesture with knobs on   200
88 Single purpose, right purpose   203
89 Pictures, photos and cartoons   205
90 Picture this, not   207
91 You cannot know it all   208
92 It takes all sorts   210
93 Draw them a diagram   214
94 Crucial modern technology   217
95 When to picture what   219
96 Multipurpose, minimal effectiveness   221
97 With a little help from your friends   223
98 Shaping up for success   225
99 Seeing is believing   227
100 A final idea   229

Afterword   231

Also by Patrick Forsyth
(and published by Cyan/Marshall Cavendish)

Detox your career: a guide to active career
management in a dynamic workplace

Manage your boss: how to create a
mutually constructive relationship

There's no need to shout!: creating powerful
communication in presentations and in writing

Outsmarting your competitors: techniques of sales
excellence to build profitable business

Surviving Office Politics: a light hearted guide to a fact
of office life that offers practical advice

And also in this same series: **100 Great Sales Ideas**
and **100 Great Time Management Idea**

And ... rather different:

First class – at last!: a light hearted volume of travel writing,
which contrasts economy and first class on
a train trip across South East Asia.

INTRODUCTION

I am the most spontaneous speaker in the world because every word, every gesture, and every retort has been carefully rehearsed.

George Bernard Shaw

PRESENTATIONS MATTER. There can be a great deal hanging on them and rarely, if one fails to work, do you get a second chance. A poor presentation can blight a plan, a proposal, a reputation... even a career. But making a good one is not easy, as a quotation from Sir George Jessel makes clear: *The human brain is a wonderful thing. It starts working the moment you are born and never stops until you stand up to speak in public.* If you identify with this all too readily, your fears and experience will only be made worse if you make a presentation without understanding what makes it work, without adequate preparation or founded only on some irrational belief that you can wing it.

Making a good one can be done however. Anyone can present in an acceptable, workmanlike way and many people find that it is something at which they can excel if they go about it in the right way. Few people are natural public speakers, and those that make it look easy tend to do so because they know the secret – they work at it.

Avoiding the nightmare

But stand up totally unprepared and, oh dear, things can go wrong. Consider: people stumble, they hesitate, and they sweat. They begin every other sentence with the superfluous word "Basically". Asked to comment on some project, they say "Um, er ... at this moment in time we are making considerable progress with the necessary administrative preliminary work prior to the establishment of the initial first phase of work" when they mean "We aim to start soon".

Just when they should be impressing their audience with their expertise and confidence, and making them interested in what they have to say, they upset or confuse them. Exactly what is said and how it is put matters; indeed there may be a great deal hanging on it. As American comedian Bob Hope used to say of his early performances, "If the audience liked you, they didn't applaud, they let you live."

At worst, people go on too long, their explanation explains nothing and where they are going is wholly unclear. Some fidget endlessly, others remain stock still gripping the table or lectern in front of them until their knuckles go white and fear rises from them like a mist. Still others are apt to pick holes in people in the audience, or their noses. If they use slides, then they can only be read from the rear of the room with a telescope, a fact made worse by their asking brightly, "Can you see alright at the back?" despite the fact that there is precious little they can do about it if the answer is "no", and in any case they should not be asking, they should know their slides are legible. They barely pause for breath as they rush from one word to the next – many of them inappropriately chosen and as many more too long. Indeed, the only long word of which some speakers appear ignorant is "rehearsal".

Of course, a lucky few believe that making a speech or presentation is second nature. They know they can wing it. They are convinced that they know their stuff and how to put it across. The first rule then for the inappropriately overconfident is, of course, to assume that the audience is as thick as they look and will, provided the right level of impenetrable gobbledegook is hit, instantly conclude that they are in the presence of a master.

They believe that winging it means that if they want people to actually understand even the gist of what is said, then a certain care must be taken. So, they talk v-e-r-y s-l-o-w-l-y, use simple words, and generally proceed on the basis that the audience have the brains of a retarded dormouse. They spell out complicated bits in CAPITAL LETTERS, speaking more loudly as they do so. Though they are always careful not to be condescending, as that will upset people (you *do know* what "condescending" *means*, don't you?).

For this kind of speaker, being on their feet is something to savor. They need only the briefest of introductions and they are away, moving quickly past the first slide without noticing that it is number twelve, the coins in their trouser pocket rattling at 90 decibels and the audience hanging on their every repetitive mannerism as they mutter to themselves, "If he scratches his backside while standing on one leg again, I'm walking out". It makes lesser mortals feel all too sadly inadequate – even the famous: it was Mark Twain who reportedly said, "It normally takes me three weeks to prepare a good impromptu speech". Poor man; just as well he was a good writer.

But even speakers convinced of their own abilities, however wrongly they hold that view, should not hog all the opportunities for themselves just because they are fun. They should give others a chance. Next time someone asks, "Will you make the presentation?" they may hand over the task to whoever displays the least enthusiasm (maybe to you?). It will do them good they think; and they may feel that there is nothing like inflicting sheer terror on a friend or colleague to make them feel superior.

Putting someone in front of an important audience, knowing that they would rather chew off their own fingers than sit and listen to someone who cannot make the simplest point clear, is rather like pushing them into a lion's den. Without an understanding of how to go about it in the right way, they will be in deep, deep trouble. No audience will warm to a speaker who is ill prepared and who flounders through a presentation that is tedious, confusing and poorly delivered. And nor will they if the speaker is poor through unthinkingly believing they can wing it. Furthermore, no poor speaker is likely to magically acquire the requisite skills instantaneously in the few seconds between being introduced, rising to their feet to speak and clicking on the mouse.

So, if you are not in fact a natural, and few people are, you need to give it some thought before you get to your feet; once you are actually in the lion's den it is a little late to discover that salvation is not guaranteed by saying, "Nice pussycat".

Maybe you should give up now. But wait a moment. Perhaps salvation is at hand. All sorts of people manage to make workmanlike presentations and many make really good ones. They have something in common. They think about it, they study it and they prepare; and they learn from experience. They make it work. Indeed there is much that can be done to avoid a presentation becoming bland and lacklustre. The approaches and ideas that follow can be used or adapted to underpin and enliven what you do and maximize its effectiveness. Dip in; as the next section states the ideas here are broadly grouped but intentionally in random order. Then, take a deep breath and begin: Good morning, everyone...

Patrick Forsyth
Touchstone & Consultancy
28 Saltcote Malting
Maldon
Essex CM9 4QP
United Kingdom

Spring 2010

THE IDEAS

The ideas led the preparation of this book.

The main criteria involved in selecting them were to describe approaches that make sense – that work – and which also demonstrate a constructive part of the total task of making a formal presentation.

Many of these ideas are no doubt in use by many different people – including me! With some (many?), although many people regard them as normal, it is also common to see them ignored. I believe that almost everything documented here can potentially be useful to most executives and managers – it is their usefulness that got them included.

Some ideas are such that they will only be relevant to certain people (for example some relate to those speaking to large audiences), but that is the nature of examples. What matters is whether they can, by their nature, assist you in making changes and doing things differently so that your impact is positively affected. So, do not reject an idea because it does not seem immediately to suit you. Look for how the idea – or just the germ of the idea – might act to add power to your presentational ability and how precisely you might be able to draw on it to deploy an approach in your own situation that will positively help you achieve what you want.

The range of ideas is intentionally eclectic. Many relate to my own experience and practice – all I have observed utilized by a range of different people with whom I have crossed paths in my training and consultancy work. All can potentially teach us something. Some ideas are self contained, affecting a moment of what you do; others can influence your whole approach. Similarly some are short, while others lead into an exposition of a complete technique best not dissected further. Some you will be able to use at once, while others may, as has been said, prompt thought that in turn leads to action and change. Some may only be interesting, but of no immediate relevance – sometimes because you are operating that way already. No matter, the process of reading the book is likely to put you in a constructive frame of mind and ultimately that is part of the process of change, a change that can affect you and how you come across in presentational mode.

Note: The ideas are arranged in an intentionally random order. This book, indeed the series of which it is part, is intended as much as anything to be dipped into. The book is divided into four sections: before, during and after the presentation, and then, separately, those ideas relating to visual aids. Note also that numbers of individual ideas relate to various common areas, for example, those concerned with making a good start.

PART 1
BEFORE YOU START

"It usually takes me three weeks to
prepare a good impromptu speech."
Mark Twain

The ideas in this first section relate to both overall matters needing consideration ahead of presenting and affecting presenting broadly, and also to the specifics of preparation.

1 THE OVERALL OPPORTUNITY

As was said in the Introduction, presentations are important. To make no bones about it, they put you in an exposed position. You stand up, start talking and the next few minutes can have a profound effect on not only whatever outcome you are aiming at (will your audience agree with you, for instance), but on your job or even career. Effective presenting is a *"career skill"** and also one that provides real opportunities; indeed a presentation has been described as the business equivalent of an open goal. Being a good presenter can achieve things and take you places. But presenting is an activity that is also:

- Fragile

- Subject to detail

Small changes, maybe only a poorly chosen phrase, word or even emphasis, can make the difference between something going well or turning into a disaster. Similarly, small differences can boost a presentation, adding a stronger emphasis, an improved impression or real power that makes ultimate overall success more likely.

The idea

The first idea here, one linked to all the others and affecting everything about how well your presentations will go across, is simply to resolve not to attempt to wing it. Study of the matter and preparation for individual presentations makes all the difference. And details matter.

In practice

- Take an interest in what makes presentations work (and fail).

- Remember that it is not a question of one single magic formula, but of letting effective details mount up.

- Always prepare and think through what you are going to do.

- Resolve to learn from experience – your own and that of others.

* Career skill is a term used and explored in my book *Detox your career* (Marshall Cavendish), which shows how such affect not just your ability to do the day to day job, but your ability to progress, from a career point of view.

2 READING ISN'T SPEAKING

S<small>OME PEOPLE THINK</small>, at least until they have more experience, that having every word down on paper and reading them out acts as a form of security blanket. After all what can go wrong if you have everything, right down to the last comma, in black and white in front of you? Well, two things in particular: you will find it is really very difficult to read anything smoothly, getting all the emphasis exactly where it needs to be, and to do so fluently and without stumbling. The actors that record novels and other books as audio works deserve their pay cheques: real skill is involved here.

The overall effect of reading, especially something you are not really familiar with, can easily sound dreary and bland; the process actually restricts your ability to make your presentation come alive rather than help it do so.

The idea

The idea here is not only to recognize that you should *not* read verbatim and avoid doing so, but also to *organize* yourself away from doing so.

In practice

* Remember that mostly, certainly in a business context, you do not need to be able to guarantee so exact a form of wording that you must read (there are exceptions, of course, a key definition or description may need to be word perfect). It is usually more

important to ensure the emphasis, variety and pace is right and that is what is so difficult to achieve when reading.

- Avoid at all costs the annoying mannerism favoured by many politicians of reading line by line (especially from the teleprompter) and ignoring punctuation, so that all the pauses are at the line end:

  "Good morning ladies and ...

  gentlemen, I am here today to give you a ...

  clear insight into our policy on ..."

- Most people speak very much better from notes which are an abbreviation of what they intend to say. If you doubt this, just try it – read something out loud and demonstrate just how it sounds; better still record it and hear how it sounds.

3 A FINAL REHEARSAL?

As IS MADE clear in many of the ideas in this first part of the book, preparation is crucial. If a presentation is to go well it will benefit from thought and planning, indeed the idea of just "winging it", even for the more experienced presenters, can spell disaster. Sometimes even careful preparation is not enough.

The idea

Where the import of what you must do, or the level of your expertise, demands it, always take the time to rehearse.

Once you have what you aim to say planned and documented in a form that you can refer to and speak from on the day, you may want to move from just thinking about and planning what you intend to do to actually trying it out – rehearsing.

In practice

- This may simply be done in your head, but may usefully involve talking through the final form out loud, or recording it on a tape-recorder (or dictating machine), or even in video form.

- While it may be sufficient to practice to the bathroom mirror as it were, it may be better to have a trial run with a sympathetic friend or colleague listening (although, on second thoughts, you may think it prudent to omit the "sympathetic"; some constructive criticism and ideas may well help, although you must ultimately decide the final form).

- Within an organization you might involve others on a swap basis. It takes some time, so if you have a colleague who can do it for you from time to time in return for your doing it for them, it is fair – and useful – to both of you.

- For anything especially important, this is a stage well worth giving some time to – not least, a complete run through, however it may be done, is the only certain way to judge whether the duration is going to be as you want it to be, at least until experience makes that judgement easier.

- Do not rule these ideas out because they may seem embarrassing. Talking to a recorder in an empty room can seem odd and awkward, but rehearsal can really help, especially at a stage when your experience is still limited.

4 YOUR "PRESENTING PROFILE"

AUDIENCES MAKE QUICK and sometimes brutal judgements. Before you have said very much at all they are passing judgement, telling themselves this will be good ... or not. Because riveting content needs time to make an impression, more must be done and there is a good deal more to it than simply sounding or appearing pleasant.

The idea

Decide on and actively present the appropriate persona. Some factors are largely common. You will probably want to include a need to appear:

- Efficient

- Approachable

- Knowledgeable (in whatever ways the audience expects)

- Well organized

- Reliable

- Consistent

- Confident

- Expert (and able to offer sound advice)

For example, people like to feel they are listening to someone competent, someone they can respect. Fair enough. Whatever the circumstances the thing to note is that there is a fair sized list of characteristics that are worth getting across, and all of them are elements that can be actively added to the mix as it were. You can *intend* to project an image of, say, confidence, and make it more than you feel; or of fairness when you want it to be absolutely clear that this is what you are being.

There is some complexity involved here and thus it is another aspect of the whole process that deserves some active consideration. Anyone, whatever their role, can usefully think through the most suitable profile for them in this way.

In practice

- It is not just personal. You personify your organization and you must often have a clear vision of how you want to project that too, and the department or function you are in for that matter. This is especially important when you are dealing with people with whom you have less regular or detailed contact, those in other departments for instance. Consider whether you should put on an appearance of:

  - Innovation

  - Long experience and substance

  - Technical competence

  - A very human face

  - Confidence

  Again you must decide on the list that suits you, and emphasize your intended characteristics as appropriate to create the total picture that is right for whoever it is to whom you communicate. This is often no more than just a slight exaggeration of a characteristic, but can still be important.

- The make up of an audience dictates the final mix. For example, some people may warm to an experienced manager with apparent concern for their staff. If so, then the qualities creating that impression can usefully be stressed. Others may seek more weight; so, a style with more examples involved makes sense for them and you will need to project appropriate clout to make it stick.

- The use of slides in presenting is an important part of what creates the right profile for the presenter. Poor slides may make presenting awkward and the audience rate what is being done lower; even a good presentation with poor slides can be less effective than it might. Both the slides themselves and whether they help the audience *matter*, so too the way they are used. A presenter who fumbles slides, forgetting to move to the next at the right moment, flitting over one as if changing their mind about including it or standing so that people in the group cannot see the screen is not going to be seen as professional.

5 SETTING OBJECTIVES

SOMETIMES PEOPLE SORT of speak about something but without real purpose, and without it really going anywhere. Even quite engagingly-delivered presentations can fail because they have no clear direction. Avoiding this demands one vital step.

The idea

To ensure a successful presentation you must set clear objectives. Objectives are not what you wish to say; they are what you wish to achieve by saying something.

For example, consider a manager addressing a staff meeting about a new policy. The task is almost certainly not simply to describe the policy; more likely it is to ensure they understand the change and how it will work, accept the necessity for it and are promptly able to undertake future work in a way that fits the new policy.

Thus such a presentation might logically comprise of five points:

- Some background to the change

- An explanation of why it is necessary (perhaps in terms of the good things it will achieve)

- Exactly what the change is and how it will work

- The effect on the individual

- What action needs to be taken and by when

To lead you to such an approach, objectives should always be, as a much quoted acronym has it, SMART. That is they should be:

- Specific

- Measurable

- Achievable

- Realistic

- Timed

In practice

- Objectives should have a clear focus on the audience. It is more important to think about what will work for them, rather than what it is that you want in isolation. Thus, to show how this works, you might regard objectives in this light for your reading of this book as:

  - To enable you to ensure your future presentations come across in a way that will be seen by your audiences as appropriate and informative (specific)

  - To ensure (measurable) action occurs afterwards (for example, the success of certain future presentations might be measured by the number of people agreeing to take certain actions after they have heard them)

  - To provide sufficient information and ideas in a manageable form for you to really be able to make a difference to what you do in future (providing an achievable objective)

  - To be not just achievable but realistic, that is, desirable (for example, the time it takes to read this book, thus taking you away from other matters, might be compared with the possible gains from so doing – if it took, say, a couple of days this might well be over-engineering)

- Timed – when are you going to review (in part by reading the book) how you go about making presentations? After all, results cannot come from such a review until it has occurred.

- Before you get up and speak you must always be able to answer questions about your presentation, such as:

  - Why am I doing this? (For example, so that people are better informed.)

  - What am I trying to achieve? (Say, to put them in a position to take, willingly and effectively, a particular action). Saying, "This is a talk about time management" is insufficient. It might be interesting, but what are the objectives? If we say, "This is a talk about time management" and extend the thought, "which means that I want people to understand the process, see it as manageable and actually be able to do things afterwards that will improve their productivity," then we are getting a lot clearer and more specific.

6   AN OVERALL STRUCTURE

PRESENTATIONS SHOULD HAVE a beginning, a middle and an end. The oldest, and perhaps the wisest, saying about the nature of communications generally is perhaps the advice to: Tell 'em, tell 'em and tell 'em. In other words you should:

- Tell people what you are going to tell them

- Tell them

- And then tell them what you have told them

It is the way, for instance, a good written report is arranged: an introduction, the body of the content and a summary. If this sounds like common sense, it is. It is also an area of common fault. I regularly see people who in other ways are good presenters, diluting the impression they make because they are following no clear structure. They ramble from one thing to the next, constantly saying things like "And also...", "Let me add...", and, at worst appearing to cobble together what they say randomly as they go. Their audience gets lost or find what is being said difficult to follow, and they end up being less impressive than they would be if what they did had a structure. Bear in mind the fact that people like to have things in context and know, at least to some extent, what is coming; they also like to find that what is said flows logically.

The idea

Adopt a structured approach. The stages – beginning, middle and end – are reviewed in various other ideas here to investigate both how they can be made to form a cohesive whole, and also how the detailed way each is handled can make them successful in putting your ideas across.

In practice

- The principle here is one that will assist preparation, keep everything organized and help hang it all together logically.

- It will also give shape to the whole presentation. Indeed it may be appropriate to note when you are moving on not just in terms of topic but of stages: "Enough by way of introduction, let's get to the meat of the matter. First..."

- The principle of the three "tell 'ems" works not only for the overall structure, but for each individual topic: anything may be presented in sufficient detail or at such length that it needs its own beginning, middle and end. Keeping organized and letting people feel that they are following a logical structure and progression acts as a safe foundation to any presentation.

7 PROVIDE YOUR OWN EXPERIENCE

Many people make presentations; some regularly, some very regularly, but some only occasionally. It is my experience that most often the presentations that must be made by those who undertake few of them are no less important than any other. But lack of experience can mean they remain in the doldrums, less than perfect, recognized as such and yet with little ongoing experience to act to boost their quality. So, and here is an idea which, if you are in this category you may not like, can speed improvement.

The idea

You must make more presentations; more specifically you must organize to make more presentations. Doing so can accelerate your experience and help you get on top of the job of making good ones.

In practice

* Seek opportunities to make more presentations. This may usefully include volunteering to make some – those that must be done by someone in your department for instance. Or it may mean volunteering for tasks which then necessitate your making presentations by their nature – becoming a member of a committee might be a good way, so too might taking on a specific role on that committee.

* Use every presentation you make as a learning experience, even if those you add are not exactly the kind of thing you need to do in your main job and tasks.

- You may also be able to collaborate with others, either asking to take over presentations they would normally make or working with others to utilize occasions so that they help. For example, in a departmental meeting it might be agreed that certain contributions will be made more formally, standing up.

- Remember, for all the study and preparation you do, there is no substitute for experience.

8 YOU AND YOUR SHADOW

Every presentation you make potentially helps you improve the standard of what you do next. But it adds more if you can glean some counselling from a more experienced presenter. In many organizations of any size there is a way in which this can be organized.

The idea

Find a presentational mentor to help you. A mentor is someone who exercises a low-key and informal developmental role. More than one person can be involved in the mentoring of a single individual and, while what they do is akin to some of the things a line manager should do, more typically in terms of how the word is used, a mentor is not your line manager. It might be someone more senior, someone on the same level or from elsewhere in the organization. An effective mentor can be a powerful force in your development. So how do you get yourself a mentor?

In practice

- In some organizations this is a regular part of ongoing development. You may be allocated one or able to request one. Equally, you may need to act to create a mentoring relationship for yourself (something that may demand a little persuasion). You can suggest it to your manager, or direct to someone you think might undertake the role, and take the initiative.

- What makes a good mentor? The person must:

- Have authority (this might mean they are senior or just that they are capable and confident)

- Have suitable knowledge and experience, counselling skills and appropriate clout

- Be willing to spend some time with you (their doing this with others may be a positive sign)

- Finding time may be a challenge. One way to minimize that problem is to organize mentoring on a swap basis: someone agrees to help you and you line up your own manager (or you for that matter) to help them, or one of their people (on the same or a different topic).

- Mentoring most usefully consists of a series of informal meetings, creating a thread of activity together through the operational activity. These meetings need an agenda (or at least an informal one), but more importantly, they need to be constructive. If they are, then one thing will naturally lead to another and a variety of occasions can be utilized to maintain the dialogue. A meeting – followed by a brief encounter as people pass on the stairs – a project and a promise to spend a moment on feedback – an e-mail or two passing in different directions – all may contribute. What makes this process useful is the commitment and quality of the mentor. Where such relationships can be set up, and where they work well, they add a powerful dimension to the ongoing cycle of development, one that it is difficult to imagine being bettered in any other way; indeed they gather strength with time and familiarity.

- Mentoring can help presenting at all stages: preparation, rehearsal, monitoring and critiquing actual presentations and planning what is done next.

MAY THE BEST MAN WIN

IT IS OFTEN said that the sheer power of a presentation can act to influence the outcome regardless of content. Thus a better presented plan may gain acceptance for a plan that is actually no better than, or even inferior to, another that is less well presented.

The idea

When your skills are such that it is viable, engineer presentations in situations where judgement might normally be made without such a formal input, so that in competitive situations your presentational power helps carry the day and get you what you want.

In practice

- This is clearly a factor in sales where competing suppliers vie to impress a potential customer, but it can be just as useful internally and may win you acceptance of plans, budgets and more that might otherwise be lost to you.

- Make the suggestion, "Perhaps it would help if I made a short presentation about this," in a low key way without it being obvious why you are doing so. Sometimes this will get someone else who initially hoped not to present having to do so alongside you, sometimes it means your case will include a presentation while a competitive pitch will not – in either case, you can create an advantage.

- It is clearly sensible to have an accurate idea of how well a competitor might perform before using this idea.

IT IS NOT JUST NERVES

PRESENTATING MAY MAKE you nervous. Be reassured: everyone has some fears. The commonest stated (I ask participants on courses I conduct) usually include (in no particular order):

- Butterflies in the stomach
- A dry mouth making it difficult to speak
- Not knowing where to put your hands
- Fear of the reaction of the audience
- Fear of not having enough material
- Fear of not being able to get through the material in the time
- Not knowing how loud to pitch your voice
- Losing your place
- Over- or under-running on time
- Being asked questions you cannot answer
- Drying up

Faced with all this, how do you cope?

The idea

Whether such things are real fears for you or just cause minor concern, the way forward is to take a practical view of the problem. There are actions that actually sort out and remove some of these problems; others are helped by the way you organize the speaking environment (dealt with in Idea 27). So what to do? Just feeling worried is difficult to combat. Ask yourself why you are worried and you may well surprise yourself; discovering that there is a practical solution to your fear that will remove or reduce whatever factor is creating the feeling and, at best, allow you to put it right out of your thoughts. The factors mentioned above are now taken in turn.

In practice

- Butterflies in the stomach: this is a physical manifestation of any worries you may have. In mild form it does no harm and fades as the adrenalin starts to flow when you get underway. On the other hand, a number of practical measures undoubtedly help reduce the feeling. Some are seemingly small, perhaps even obvious; but they are effective, however, and may work better when several are used together. They include:

  - A few deep breaths just before you start

  - No heavy food too soon before you start

  - No starvation diets, or the butterflies will be accompanied by rumbles

  - No alcohol (some would say very little) before you start

  - Plus the confidence of knowing you are well prepared and organized

- Dry mouth: again this is a natural reaction, but one easily cured. Just take a sip of water before you start. The longer the duration of your talk, the more you will need to take the occasional sip. Talking makes you dry and an air-conditioned room compounds the problem. Act accordingly, throughout your talk.

- Somewhere to put your hands: somehow they can feel awkward. They seem like disproportionately large lumps at the end of your arms. The trick here is to avoid obvious awkwardness. Give yourself something to do with them – hold a pen perhaps – and then forget about them.

- Audience reaction: or rather the fear of a negative one. Ask yourself why they would react negatively. The fear may be irrational. It may be because you feel ill prepared. And also remember that audiences hate poor presentations; they want you to succeed.

- Not having enough material: this should simply not be a fear. Your preparation will mean you know you have not only enough but the right amount of material for the topic and the time.

- Having too much material: this needs no separate comment from the previous point except that even if you start with too much, preparation should whittle it down to the appropriate amount.

- Not knowing how loud to speak: this may be a reasonable fear in a strange room, but you can test it; if in doubt just talk to the back row.

- Losing your place: again there are practical measures to help. Know your message well, particularly in terms of the exact format of the speaker's notes that you opt to have in front of you.

- Misjudging the timing: in part an accurate judgement of time comes with practice. If you find it difficult, do not despair, you will get better and better at it. Link your notes to timing and watch the clock.

- Being asked questions you cannot answer: no one is expected to be omniscient. Here let me make the one point that it is not the end of the world to say: "I don't know" – always an important point for any would-be presenter to accept (although you might have to make some further comment; maybe "I'll find out and get back to you.").

- Drying up: here one must address the reason why this might happen. Dry mouth? Sip of water. Lost your place? If that does not happen because your notes are easy to follow, you will not dry up. Just nerves? Well, some of the elements mentioned elsewhere – and preparation – will help. It is worth remembering here that time often seems to flow at a different rate for presenters and audiences. A pause as you collect your wits may seem long, yet hardly be noticed by your audience.

11 THE RIGHT SORT OF CRIB

However experienced, most people like to have a note of some sort in front of them as guidance and insurance against drying up. However much you may need this and however much you need it on the day, it has to allow you to work from it conveniently and with certainty.

The idea

Pick a form of speaker's note that suits both you and the nature of the occasion. The details of exactly what to have on your notes and in what detail and form are dealt with separately; here the first step is to pick the right overall form.

In practice

- The form you adopt must suit you, be legible, easy to follow visually, and easy to manage too so that you can work with no distraction or worry.

- That said, the form must suit the occasion:

  - If you are to speak from a lectern, then A4 papers may be fine. Put them in a ring binder and they will lie flat and you could have notes on one side of a double page spread and reproductions of slides on the other.

  - A binder works well if you are at a table, although the size of the typeface of writing needs to be larger as your eyes will be further away from the page as you stand than when sitting at your desk.

- If you must move around, or for any reason have nothing to stand behind, then a clipboard may suit (make sure that the pages turn over smoothly), although some presenters prefer cards (postcard size or a bit larger).

- Whatever you use make sure the pages are secure and numbered – and beware turning over two pages at once, which can have you remembering what to say but still not making sense!

12 TIME WELL SPENT

MOST ORGANIZATIONS, AND most readers of this book, are busy. There never seems to be enough time for anything; deadlines are plentiful and impossible, and levels of stress rise by the hour. Another volume in this series addresses this problem (*100 Great Time Management Ideas*) and you may want to investigate how you can improve your productivity separately. Here I recommend you making and keeping one resolution.

The idea

Never, ever skimp the time it takes to prepare a presentation. Do not think you can wing it. Any shortfall in preparation will show; it can be damaging and, at worst, can prove fatal to your intentions, your effectiveness, your reputation, and even your career.

I have long since lost count of the times I have heard people bemoan the fact that "there was not enough time to prepare"; it's almost as if they believe that this excuses making a poor presentation. Yet skimping wastes more time: for instance, if a presentation to a potential customer fails to impress, you have not just lost the time it took – you have to invest more time and effort to get another prospect to the same stage.

In practice

- Use every trick in the book to make time to prepare presentations properly: extend the deadline, rearrange the priorities, beg or blackmail colleagues to let you offload something on them – whatever it takes.

- Link this principle to rehearsal if that is necessary (see Idea 3).

- Finally, if there are inadequacies (and you will gather I do not think there should be) then do not apologize for them or otherwise draw attention to them. Saying, "Ideally I would have some slides, however time ruled this out, let's see if we can manage without..." is hardly likely to get an audience labelling you "professional". You are better off just proceeding and just making it as good as it can be without comment.

13 A BEAR OF VERY LITTLE BRAIN

THERE IS ONE factor regarding preparation that should be spelt out clearly – the advantage of a systematic approach; which, for most people, is a great help. I like to think I am reasonably adept at many things but I also know that if I try to do, or concentrate on, too much at once I become muddled. A systematic approach to preparation helps avoid this danger and one simple trick plays a big part in this.

The idea

As you prepare, separate two key yet different tasks: concentrate first on the content, what you will say, and only secondly move on to *how* you will put it across.

Perhaps I am a simple soul, but I find this easier than simply looking at what I must do sequentially, and trying to work out *what* I need to say and *how* I can best put it across at the same time. If it is easier to work this way, it is likely to be quicker to prepare also. Better speeches in less time seem like a good reason for going about the preparation process in a systematic way.

In practice

- Avoid a sequential approach (preparation that simply thinks through what you will say and how you will put it together), where you start with "Ladies and gentlemen..." and move on from there. Content first, manner of delivery next should be the order of the day.

- Many details about making a presentation reviewed throughout this book will reinforce the need for careful preparation. There is a good deal to think about. But there is no reason why, with practice, the process of assembling a talk should not be accomplished in a reasonable amount of time.

However, to begin with at least, do not skimp on preparation. There is a good deal to think about, and even a short talk demands care and attention. Incidentally, some would say that this is *especially* so with a short talk, and certainly in a few short minutes any faults will stand out sharply and small details can have a disproportionate impact for both good and ill.

PUTTING YOUR MESSAGE TOGETHER

IT IS NOT only necessary to "engage the brain before the mouth", but also vital to think through – in advance – what a presentation must contain, and not contain, for that matter. The following process of thinking through and preparing is recommended solely for its practicality and can be adapted to cope with any sort of presentation, of any length or complexity, and of any purpose. Many communications fail or their effectiveness is diluted because preparation is skimped on; give it the necessary time.

In the long run preparation saves time, in part on the old premise that while there is never time to do things properly, there always has to be time made available to sort out any mess caused by an inadequate approach.

The idea

Adopt a systematic approach to preparing a presentation; it will allow you to be ready more quickly and ensure that what you then have is ready for effective delivery. How does this work?

In practice

- **Stage 1 – Listing**: Forget about everything such as sequence, structure, and arrangement; just concentrate on and list – in short note (or keyword) form – every significant point that the presentation might usefully contain. Give yourself plenty of space (an extra large piece of paper lets you see everything at one glance). Set down the points as they occur to you, almost at random across the page. For something simple this might result only in a dozen words, or it might be far more. You will find that this process is a good thought prompter. It enables you to fill out the picture as one thought leads to another, with the freestyle approach removing the need to pause to link points or worry about sequence. With this done, you have a full picture of the possibilities for the message in front of you as you move on.

- **Stage 2 – Sorting**: Now, you can review what you have noted down and begin to bring some order to it, deciding:

  - What comes first, second and so on

  - What logically links together, and how

  - What provides evidence, example, or illustration to your points?

  - At the same time, you can – and probably will – add some additional things and have second thoughts about other items, deleting as well as amending the wording a little if necessary. You need to bear in mind the intended duration and prune as necessary. This stage can often be completed rapidly just by simply annotating and amending the first stage document (use a second color, link lines, arrows etc., to make things clear). Here you can begin to capture more detailed elements as you go through (content and presentational style), noting what it is on the page or alongside.

- **Stage 3 – Arranging**: Sometimes, at the end of stage 2, you have a note that is sufficiently clear and from which you can work to finalize matters. If it can benefit from clarification, however, it may be worth rewriting as a neat list or into the format you adopt for your speaking notes; or this could be the stage where you type it and put it on screen if you are working that way and want to be able to print something out in due course. Final revision is possible as you do this, certainly you should be left with a list reflecting the content, emphasis, level of detail, and so on that you feel is appropriate. You may well find you are pruning a bit to make things more manageable at this stage, rather than searching for more content and additional points to make.

- **Stage 4 – Reviewing**: This may be unnecessary. Sufficient thought may have been brought to bear through earlier stages. However, for something particularly complex or important (or both) it may be worth running a final rule over your plan. Sleep on it first perhaps – certainly avoid finalizing matters for a moment if you have gotten too close to it. It is easy to find you cannot see the wood for the trees. Make any final amendments to the list (on screen it is a simple matter) and use this as your final "route map" as preparation continues.

- **Stage 5 – Prepare the "message"**: For a presentation this would be in the form of speaker's notes. Now you can turn your firm intentions about content into something representing not only what will be said, but also how you will put it across. This stage must be done carefully, although the earlier work will have helped to make it easier and quicker to get the necessary details down.

- **Stage 6 – A final check**: A final look (perhaps after a break) is always valuable. This is also the time to consider rehearsal; something dealt with elsewhere (in Idea 3).

15 SPEAKER'S NOTES: A SUGGESTED FORMAT

You NEED TO develop a good system for creating the material you will have in front of you on the day. Doing so has real benefits. For instance, you won't lose your way. You will remember to show the next slide at the right moment and give different points the emphasis you intend. Let's see how this works, and look at how much material you need to note down, what an effective format should feature, and how you get the key points to jump out at you as you speak. For instance, you need to decide how detailed your notes need to be.

The idea

Consider a practical format and style in which to set out your notes. You may experiment with suggestions described here and adapt it, but then stick with it so that your standard form assists you to work well – at a glance. The detailed suggestions below are worth a try.

In practice

- The detail here must be sufficient to give you – being otherwise well prepared – something easy to follow.

- Certainly *color* makes a difference to the clarity of notes and can be used in a number of ways: if certain elements stand out in, say, red, it does help (as well as devices such as highlighting, underlining, and bullet points). In this way, the eye can quickly focus on each element without too much conscious effort.

- The page is usefully ruled (use color here) into 2-3 smaller blocks that are each of a size that is easier to focus on as you look to and fro from the audience to the page (this works on an A4 page, though its content could equally be spread over 2-3 cards).

- Symbols are used for example, to show there is a slide to put on (a bold **S3** and so on), or a need to pause (///////). Always use the same symbol for the same thing or you may find yourself puzzling over what they mean.

- Columns can be used to separate main headings from the body of the notes and leave room for additional material (I like three: main headings on the left, the detail in the centre and "options" – see Idea 24 – on the right).

- Emphasis can be shown (again color does this best).

- Text should be spaced out (to allow further amendment and make it easier to focus on), and if typed, sufficiently large to read as you stand up.

- Timing can be mentioned (this can repeat through the piece).

- Each page must be numbered (one day they will get dropped!).

- Remember you should think carefully about what suits you best and evolve a personal style that works for you. It is worth a little experiment to achieve this. The end result can be typed, or handwritten, or be a mixture of both.

MAXIMIZING THE EFFECTIVENESS OF PREPARATION

As YOU PREPARE (systematically – see Idea 13 and 14), you need to give yourself the best chance of your preparation allowing you to produce the best presentation possible. In part, this is down to how you go about it – the systematic approach – but other factors are important and can help too.

The idea

In a busy, hectic life in which finding time for preparation may seem difficult (although it must be found), pick the time you do find wisely and consider how you use it.

In practice

- If possible, choose the right moment. There seem to be times when your thoughts flow more easily than others (this shows as you talk it through to yourself). Certainly, interruptions can disrupt the flow and make the process take much longer, as you recap and restart again and again. The right time – uninterrupted time in a comfortable environment (which may well need organizing) – always helps.

- Keep going. Do not pause and agonize over some small detail. You can always come back to something, indeed it may even be easier to complete later. If you keep going you maintain the flow, allowing consistent thinking to carry you through the structure to the end so that you can "see" the overall shape of it. Once you have the main details down, then you can go back and fine-tune, adding any final thoughts to complete the picture.

A GUIDING HAND

HAVING SOMETHING CLEAR and simple to follow as a guide boosts confidence; it acts like a firm hand on the tiller, assisting you to maintain direction and aiding control (and also facilitating digression where that may be appropriate). The trick is not to write out the speech verbatim,but rather to reflect the skeleton of the material, prompt particular factors – from moments of emphasis, such as a dramatic pause, to using a visual of some sort – and to remind you of the detail against the background of a clear structure.

The idea

It is worth evolving a specific format for your speaker's notes that suits you. There is no need to follow anyone else's ideas unless they suit you – although take what is useful from wherever you may come across it. If you use the same broad approach consistently it speeds preparation, and assists monitoring time as you get to know how long a page or card in your personal style represents in terms of delivery time.

In practice

- Notes provide a foundation for your presentation and a helping hand along the way. Here are some general principles (more details about format appear in Idea 15):

  - Notes must be legible (use a sufficiently large size of typeface or writing), and not just when you are sitting at your desk, but when on your feet.

- Ensure notes will stay flat as you use them on the day (an A4 ring binder may be best, or cards loosely linked with a tie-cord).

- Using only one side of the paper allows amendment and addition if necessary (or if you are using a fair number of slides then a copy of these might go alongside your notes).

- Always number the pages – you do not want to get lost (and you would not be the first to drop your notes if disaster strikes). Some people like doing the numbering in reverse, with the last page being number one – the countdown effect acts to provide information about how much material and time you have remaining as you proceed.

- Separate graphically different kinds of instruction and material (for example, making clear what you will say and also indicating something about how you will say it).

- Use color and symbols to provide emphasis.

18 I THINK, THEREFORE I FAIL...

Most, if not all, of the problems you may anticipate in speaking formally can be removed or reduced by preparation.

Preparation can quite literally make the difference between success and failure, and can turn something routine into something memorable.

The idea

As part of your preparation, "talk your way to success" – think positively.

In practice

- Psychologists say that more than seventy per cent of what is called "self-talk" about speaking formally is negative. This refers to all those thoughts that start with: "I'm not sure I can..." or "It won't be..." Understandable perhaps, but doubts can all too easily become a self-fulfilling prophecy and many that arise in this way are intangible and not factually based. You need to combat this by thinking positively. Imagine it going well. Visualize the detail of particular elements working as you planned. Do so repeatedly and beat negative thoughts into submission (having addressed and solved any specific and tangible problems). Why not imagine the applause too?

- The time for this thinking is as you prepare. And bear in mind that the single most common reason why things sometimes do not go well is because the person concerned gave insufficient time to preparation. Bear in mind too that, quite simply, what you do in preparing creates the certainty that it will go well.

- So the rule should be: Prepare – Practice – Present, and think positive. If the practical issues are addressed, you can then put irrational fears on one side, recognizing them for what they are.

19 WHEN THE ORDER OF THE DAY IS MOB HANDED

LINKED TO THE subject of preparation, there is the matter of team presentations to be touched on. When a complete presentation is made up of segments with perhaps two, three or more people contributing separate parts of it, the need for preparation is magnified.

Team presentations must not only go across well, they must also appear seamless. There should be neither any disruption to the smooth flow of the content, nor any fumbling in terms of handover between speakers. Those in the audience will read any uncertainty as unprofessional. It will seem to be either a sign of bad planning or appear as a lack of respect for the audience – or both. Even if the individual presentations are good, any fumbling on handover – "I think that's all I have to say, John you were going to pick things up here, weren't you?" – will dilute effectiveness.

The idea

Make sure that the group get together to plan/rehearse. It really is extremely difficult for a group of people to present effectively together without getting together beforehand to thrash out the details. Yes, the time and pressures within many an organization may typically conspire to make such meetings difficult to arrange, but there is no substitute for them.

In practice

- You need to consider and agree on such matters as:

  - What order people will speak in (and whether this in any way should relate to the hierarchy involved – often it should not)

  - Who will be "in charge"

  - Who will speak first, second and so on

  - How speaking styles will match or detract

  - Who will organize and take questions

  - The implications for the timing

- Always allow time for joint preparation. A word or two on the telephone or a couple of e-mails is just not the same, and you liaise in this way at your peril. You have been warned.

PART 2

DURING THE PRESENTATION

"The golden rule for all presenters is
to imagine that you are in the audience."
David Martin

In this part the ideas relate to all aspects of delivery.

FIRST IMPRESSIONS LAST

FIRST IMPRESSIONS, MENTIONED more than once in these pages, are quick and powerful. In a few moments people can warm to your address or dismiss the next half hour out of hand as a guaranteed waste of time. It would be a foolish presenter that ignored this fact and it starts before you even open your mouth.

The idea

Look the part: that means having an appearance which the audience associates with authority, expertise or whatever it is that is trying to be projected, rather than what the speaker regards as comfortable or fashionable.

I would not presume to say much more about how you should look, still less how you should dress, but I would suggest you consider objectively what a powerful part of your own assessment of others this is, and then act appropriately yourself.

In practice

- Look organized: rushing to the front and spilling papers from an untidy heap of files clutched inadequately to your chest will not say "professional". Aim to come across as a good presenter – because poor presentation skills can lead to other weaknesses, including those not directly associated with presentations.

- Consider details: is your hair straight, are your shoelaces tied safely, your fingernails clean and your spectacles to hand? Omissions in these areas are quickly "marked down".

- Have respect for every audience in everything – from a seemingly reliable ability to stick to time, to a concentration on what they will find interesting and the most appropriate way to put it across. Once you open your mouth and actually go on to be clear and interesting (or any other objective the audience would wish you to deploy), appearance and expertise combine to produce a powerful image.

21 GETTING OFF TO A GOOD START

YOU CANNOT OVERESTIMATE the importance of a good start. Remember the old saying: there is only one chance to make a good first impression. The beginning is the introduction; it must set the scene, and state the topic and theme (and maybe the reason for the whole thing). Do so clearly, and get into the 'meat' of the message without too much delay. The introduction must get the group's attention and carry people along – and link into the middle and the main section and message of the talk. And to do all this it must establish some sort of rapport between the speaker and audience (see Idea 54) and get their attention.

The idea

Take active steps to get early attention. Two things assist here: your manner and the actual start you make. Your manner must get people saying to themselves: *This should be interesting, I think they know what they are talking about*. Here a confident manner pays dividends. It removes doubts and creates a positive feel. But you must still find an appropriate starting point.

In practice

Some examples of different starts are:

- **News**: something you know they do not know (and will want to): "Gentlemen, we have hit the target. I heard just as I came into the meeting, and..."

- **Something not a lot of people know, or a startling or weird fact**: "The next generation of computers, being made now in Japan, can perform ten quadrillion calculations every second. A quadrillion, incidentally, is a number followed by 18 noughts." The same effect might be obtained with something spoof: "There are two kinds of people in the world, those that divide people into categories, and the rest..."

- **A question**: actual or rhetorical and ideally designed to get people responding (at least in their minds): "How would you like to...?"

- **A quotation**: whether famous or what a member of the group said yesterday. If it makes a point, generates a smile or links firmly to the topic this can work well: "It was Oscar Wilde who said: 'There is only one thing in the world worse than being talked about, and that is not being talked about.'" (useful to introduce the public relations plan, perhaps)

- **A story or anecdote**: perhaps again to make a point, maybe something people know: "We all remember the moment when the...", or something they do not: "Last week in Singapore I got caught in the rain and..."

- **A fact**: preferably a striking one or maybe challenging, thought-provoking or surprising: "Research shows that if we give a customer cause to complain, they are likely to tell ten other people, but if we please them they will only tell one. Not a ratio to forget because..."

- **Drama**: something that surprises or shocks, or in some way delivers a punch: "The next ten minutes can change your life. It can..."

- **A gesture**: something people watch and which gets their attention: "Some people in this company seem to think that money grows on trees..." – said while tearing up a bank note and scattering the pieces.

- **History**: this may be a general historical fact or one that evokes a common memory: "Five years ago, when we all knew we were at a turning point..."

- **Curiosity**: an oddity, something that will surprise and have people waiting (perhaps eagerly) for the link with what is going to be said. It may be really odd or just out of context: "Now you may wonder why I should start with a reference to pachyderms; you may even wonder what it is." (It is a thick-skinned quadruped; apparently irrelevant but...)

- **Shock**: something totally unexpected, maybe seemingly inappropriate, that really makes people listen (though its relevance should be clear as you proceed): "Imagine this room full of dead bodies. It is a horrific thought, yet far more people than would fit in this room die every month from..." (linked to something about charities, perhaps).

- **Silence**: this may seem a contradiction in terms but can be used: "Please all remain absolutely quiet for a moment..." The speaker counts silently to ten and the gap begins to seem rather long. "That's how long it seems to customers waiting for Technical Support to answer the telephone, and it is too long."

- **A checklist**: this can spell out what is coming and there are certainly worse starts than that: "There are four key issues I want to raise today. These are..."

Such devices are not mutually exclusive. They may be used in a variety of combinations and the above list is not exhaustive. Whatever you use, remember that the impact may come from several sentences rather than something as short as the examples used above. The first words, however, do need some careful thought and must be delivered in a way that achieves exactly the effect you are after.

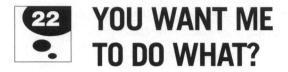

YOU WANT ME TO DO WHAT?

OVER THE YEARS I have been asked to speak at a large number of events, from major business conferences to corporate and sales meetings, with numbers attending ranging from just a couple of dozen to large crowds (my largest ever audience was around 2500; the room seemed to disappear into the distance). Unlike training sessions these are often quite short, usually somewhere in the 30 minutes to a couple of hours bracket. It is always a challenge to do justice to what is often a wide brief in a short span of time.

More often than one might think, the invitation is, well let's describe what I mean: "I wonder if you would be available to speak at our annual sales conference? It's on 31 May in Cambridge. An hour or so if you can." So far so good, I say yes and ask what the conference is about. It's our annual sales conference, they say. Great, but I ask why they are holding it and am told, "Well it's a year since we got the team together, and well we need to... stimulate them in some way." On the one hand perhaps any topic will do, on the other hand a clearer objective would be helpful.

The idea

Whatever you are asked to speak on, make sure you get a clear brief. A lack of clarity of purpose may seem to make things easier, but it also makes it easier to misjudge matters and find yourself doing something inappropriate.

In practice

- With presentations that you initiate there is no problem (or if there is, it is with you), you set the objectives and you thus know exactly what they are.

- When you are invited study the brief carefully and, if it is not entirely clear, ask for clarification. No one is likely to mind; indeed your sensible questions are likely to make you sound professional. Who are the audience? What is the objective (in terms of what the session should achieve)? What prior experience do people have of the topic? What are their expectations likely to be? So ask clear questions and press the point if necessary.

- Check too the other information you will need, from the venue to the timing and details like where you will be able to park.

SPEAKING IN TONGUES

More people may speak English in the world than any other language (until Chinese overhauls it), but many speak other languages. At certain events where the presenter and audience speak different languages, translation is provided. Seems simple: you talk, they translate – not so. It can be an odd and difficult experience.

The idea

Always make allowances for the fact of translation; your presentation must be made to go well despite this being done and some things may have to be different from the way they would when everything is in English.

In practice

- Start your consideration as you prepare: you will find translation always takes some time and to hit your timing, you may say a little less than usual and you may want to keep language, vocabulary and so on a little simpler than usual.

- Aim to meet the translator before you start to check any key words and descriptions. In a business presentation, for instance, you do not want the word "advertising" translated as "promotion".

- Make sure before you start that you can see the translator and keep an eye on them. Many languages take longer to make a point than is the case in English; German for instance is about 25% longer. You need to watch and make sure that you are not running ahead of the translator, as the quality of their translation deteriorates in their rush to keep up.

- Otherwise, aim to largely forget it and certainly not allow it to distract you.

24 THE MERITS OF A THIRD COLUMN

Whenever you are presenting and however carefully you have prepared, you may recognize the need for some change along the way. This can present difficulties as you have to think about what to add, change or omit as you go, while you are actually speaking, and it is easy to stumble. One idea linked to the format of speaker's notes (see Idea 15) helps prepare you for this.

The idea

The format of speakers' notes can usefully be in three columns: main heading down the left hand side of a page, the main prompts for your presentation in the centre – the widest column – and a third, right hand column to encompass this idea. Put a series of "Options" alongside your running order to anticipate and facilitate some fine-tuning as you go.

In practice

- Put "options" in column three that can be used, or not, as time and circumstances allow, something that can be very useful to both timing and fine-tuning; perhaps in light of an audience's reaction. The idea here is that the main content, and say, half the options, will give you the duration you want. You then decide as you go along which of these to use. Such "options" can be a valuable device, and inject a considerable element of flexibility into what you do; it helps you keep to time and maximize the impact you make.

- Use this to add:

  - Additional detail that might be required (and perhaps indicated by puzzled looks)

  - Extra examples, designed to illustrate and explain what you are talking about

  - Digressions: those with a purpose that add something useful

  - Further anecdotal elements to enhance or enliven the message

AGAIN AND
AGAIN AND...

ONE OF THE things most presenters want to achieve in most circumstances is making a message stick. They do not just want to inform or entertain; they want to have a more lasting effect – changing views or behavior or prompting action to be taken later.

The idea

The idea is to repeat things. Repetition is a fundamental help to grasping a point. Repetition is a fundamental help to... sorry. But it is true. It does not imply just saying the same thing, in the same words, repeatedly. Repetition takes a number of forms. You do not want to overdo this principle but to use it judiciously.

In practice

- Repetition can be used in a variety of ways, for instance:

  - Things being repeated in different ways (or at different stages of the same presentation)

  - Points made in more than one manner: for example, being spoken and written down (in a handout or on a slide)

  - Using summaries or checklists to recap key points

  - Reminders over a period of time (maybe varying the method – phone, email or meetings that follow up a presentation)

- Slides are essentially a form of repetition. You hear something and you see something. More than that: at a presentation, you may have considerable repetition:

  - An agenda sent in advance makes a general point

  - The introduction starts from the general (prior to moving to the particular)

  - A point is made (maybe more than once)

  - A slide is shown about it

  - An example or anecdote is used to illustrate it (maybe with a summary point at the end, or even another slide)

  - A summary mentions the point again (with another slide, perhaps)

  - A handout mentions it in writing (and includes copies of slides used)

- This is a fair bit of repetition. It can be overdone of course (perhaps as in the introduction to this point here), but it is also a genuinely valuable aid to getting the message across, especially when used with the other factors now mentioned.

- Never forget: people really are more likely to retain what they take in when they see or hear it more than once, and in different ways. (Okay, enough repetition!)

26 WIRED FOR SOUND

PEOPLE NEED TO hear you. People want to hear you (or you hope they do). And sometimes this is not possible without electronic assistance; you need a microphone.

The idea

It may seem awkward but use a microphone if it is necessary, and use it carefully.

In practice

- Despite the potential awkwardness (or the perceived awkwardness), do not avoid using a microphone when it is really necessary. Either you will alienate half the audience who cannot hear properly, or you will have to start again.

- Always test a mike beforehand to see not only that the audience will be able to hear, but that you know how loud you need to speak (you should not have to raise your voice unnaturally, but it should accommodate a louder tone if you need this for emphasis). Move heaven and earth to achieve this. If it is impossible then use two starts – "Let me just check this before I start." – to make sure all is well before you really get going.

- The most difficult thing about microphones is remembering to stay the right distance from them; practice really helps here. The problem does not have to occur these days as you can often have a tiny microphone clipped to your lapel, connected to a radio device that goes in your pocket or on your belt. If this is positioned correctly then you can just forget about it.

- Finally, a warning: microphones have an on/off switch and there are moments (as you mutter to the Chair that you would rather be anywhere else perhaps) when it needs to be off!

27 ORGANIZING THE ENVIRONMENT

CONSIDER THE SPEAKING environment, the room and particularly the immediate area you inhabit at the front of the room. If you work to ensure you are comfortable with all the arrangements that affect you, there is at once much less to distract your mind as you speak; all your thoughts can then focus on the job in hand. If not... well imagine some of the hazards of this sort: a narrow table, inadequate space, electric wires underfoot, a water jug perched on a saucer and a... enough. Anything less than ideal distracts.

The idea

Creating the right environment needs thought and planning, and the precise arrangement will depend on the circumstances and such things as whether there is a lectern, but you can and should create an arrangement as near to your ideal as any individual situation allows.

It may be worth your making a short checklist of the things that are important to the kind of presentation you have to make, and the location(s) in which you usually find yourself conducting them.

In practice

- First, prior selection and arrangement of key physical factors get things organized. Decide whether you want to use a lectern or not, if the equipment is in the right place (projector, flipchart or anything else necessary) and is tested and working, hazards are noted, removed or taped down (as with electric wires), and water jug and glass are safely placed. See if you have sufficient space for all you want to do (lay out notes, slides and so on) and know what the acoustics are like.

- Other things may be necessary too. For instance, is there a clock you can see? (If not you may want to take off your wristwatch and lay it in front of you to avoid looking visibly – pointedly – at it on your wrist.) Can you easily see any necessary signals from the Chair? Can you signal to anyone necessary (someone at the back who will summon the refreshments)? What about your microphone if there is one (see Idea 26)? Note that certain things need organizing differently depending on whether one is left or right-handed. To show slides neatly, being right-handed, I need to stand to the left of the controls (as I face them and the audience). This is a factor to watch out for, especially if you are at an outside venue. PowerPoint and OHP operation is similarly affected.

- Organize anything you personally find creates comfort for you (it does not matter if others are left cold by them) or that you just like – what you might think of as personal comfort factors. For example, I find I speak regularly from behind a standard height table. Fine, one of reasonable width usually gives plenty of room for notes, slides, projector and more. But if I lay any notes I have flat on the table then I cannot see them clearly if they are in standard-sized type. I wear spectacles and have found that if I lay a good sized, hard briefcase on the table and put notes on that, just four to six inches higher, then I can focus at a glance and, from the perspective of the audience, do not appear to be looking down so much. It suits me, looks fine and is easy to arrange.

- Don't let perfect organization become a fetish. Conditions often cannot be perfect and that must not throw you, but knowing you have things sorted as you like as much as possible can be an antidote to nerves.

- Note too that going into an unfamiliar room just before you speak is to be avoided if possible. Don't simply assume all will be well. Check and arrange matters if it is within your control and ask others, a Chairman perhaps, if it is not. People are usually disposed to help.

- Finally, always be flexible and take whatever action you can to allow you to adapt to varying conditions. For example, if speaking from a normal height table, I tend to have notes in a ring binder. However, if I assume this and find I am at a small lectern, with no room for the binder, or simply have to stand up out in the open, I always have a solid card in my folder and a bulldog clip – I can take out the notes, arrange them on a clipboard and stand holding them safely in one hand. Again, preparation and practice enable you to develop such solutions based on experience.

28 MANY, MANY, MANY...

Initially, most people have a clearly graduated reaction to the number of people in the audience. A few are not so bad – you can equate them to a round table meeting, more begins to seem more difficult; and a large number soon becomes "a terrifying sea of faces". Why so? After all, the job of the speaker is one that is very similar regardless of the numbers present. Not only may you have a similar message to get across, but to a large extent, you need to do it in a similar way.

The idea

Regard the best rule for talking to a large group as treating it like a smaller one.

Of course, you need to double-check certain things carefully with a large group (for example, the microphone or the acoustics), but otherwise relax and do not let it worry you. It is, in any case, the kind of thing that usually proves more worrying before you do it, than it does while you are doing it. If you present appropriately to the subject, the occasion and the audience, then the number present need not change things greatly.

In practice

- A number of things helps you deal with a large group, for example:

  - Eye contact is important, and with a larger group the scale of applying it is larger too, but the principle is identical.

- Be yourself. This is important for any presentation. You may want to exaggerate a little, and an expansive gesture may need to be that little more expansive in a packed conference room, but do not change your basic style because of the numbers. It is easier for you to be natural and the impression given is better for the audience.

- Use feedback. If there are more people there will be more of it; somewhere in the audience there will be an enthusiastic response to focus on.

- Use involvement. Of course, the appropriate level of formality varies, but there is no real reason not to say: "What do you think about this?" and prompt a comment or three from an audience of a hundred just as you would from one of a dozen. Similarly, you can focus on individuals even in a crowd if that is appropriate – "John Black is here somewhere. Where are you John? And what do you think?" – especially if they will appreciate it (and I am tempted to add sometimes too mischievously when they will not).

- Do not let sheer numbers put you off anything that the presentation needs, for example if you need to pause... pause, do not let the pressure of many eyes make you spoil what may be an important emphasis.

- Think of the total audience in sub-section, use eye contact to focus on small groups within the audience, then pretend that you are talking to just the six at the back or the three in the front row.

- Everyone in any group is an individual. Talk to them as individuals and there is no reason why they should not all be satisfied.

29 CLEAR INTENTIONS

A PRESENTATION THAT does not know where it is going is never going to get there, and an audience is always going to be unsatisfied with one that is such. This is surely axiomatic and there are numerous implications. Here is very much the first.

The idea

Be very clear about what you are going to do. This (see Idea 5 about setting objectives) demands some broad thinking about intentions. Do you want your presentation to:

- Inform
- Explain or instruct
- Motivate
- Persuade
- Prompt debate
- Demonstrate
- Build on past messages or dialogue with members of the audience?

In practice

- The intentions on such a list (and by all means, add to it) are not mutually exclusive. You may want to do some or all of these, or to add other intentions to the list. The point here is that, however many things of this sort there are to do, it makes preparation and delivery easier if you are clear about them all at the outset. You certainly do not want to be busy informing people and then suddenly think, *I really should be enthusing them a bit too.* It is difficult to suddenly start to try to address a newly thought of intention halfway through a talk. So, think this through at the beginning and prepare and deliver accordingly.

30 A HANDY GLASS

This idea combines a clear, simple do and also a don't.

The idea

Do and don't drink: to be specific, do drink water and be very wary of alcohol (the more so if you are nervous).

In practice

- Always have a glass of water to hand and where there is a chairman or other organizer involved, never be shy of asking for one if necessary (after all who would say, or think, *how preposterous, how dare they ask that?*); have still rather than fashionably fizzy water – the latter has side effects.

- Similarly, never apologize or put off taking a sip if you become dry; better a brief "excuse me" and a sip – time that no one will notice – rather than a real cough or dry mouth later.

- Resist the urge to have a massive gin and tonic, or anything else alcoholic for that matter, before you start. You may think it will quell nerves – you may even think it is doing so as you stand up – but it is more likely to do harm than good. At worst it may make your mouth take off and run ahead of your brain in a way that leads only to chaos.

31 THE AUDIENCE

AUDIENCES WANT THINGS to go well. But they are not totally forgiving and they will have expectations. Above all they want you to talk to them or discuss with them, not to talk at them.

The idea

Keep the audience viewpoint in mind. Like preparation, this is another near "magic" formula for success. It is one that should, of course, affect your preparation as well as your delivery and manner.

Any audience faced with the receiving end of a formal talk thinks ahead – a process that may perhaps be colored by experience of bad or boring presentations they have attended in the past. They try to guess what it will be like. They wonder if it will be interesting, amusing, or useful or just short. Whatever the intention is, they wonder if it will be achieved. They look for clues to what it will be like even before you start, which is why things like appearance, starting on time, being seen to be organized and comfortable with the proceedings are all important. In training for instance, people are asking questions such as: does this person know his subject? Will they be able to put it across? And will they do so in an interesting manner, and, if they do, will it help me? Each member of a group is an individual: they are concerned above all with themselves, and the good speaker appears to address individuals, not some amorphous entity called 'the audience'. So everything you do must reflect a focus on the audience.

In practice

- They want to find what is said understandable, interesting and a good fit with the audience and the occasion. Specifically, they want you to:

  - "Know your stuff"

  - Look the part

  - Respect them and acknowledge their situation and views

  - Make what you say link to what they want from the talk

  - Give them sufficient information to make a considered judgement about what you say (they will weigh up your views, especially if they are going to be required to take some action after you finish speaking)

  - Make them understand by the time you finish what action, if any, is needed or expected of them

- Conversely, they do not want to be:

  - Confused

  - Blinded by science, technicalities or jargon

  - Lost in an overcomplicated structure (or lack of one)

  - Talked down to

  - Made to struggle to understand inappropriate language

  - Made to make an enormous jump to relate what is said to their own circumstance

  - Listening to someone whose lack of preparation makes it clear that they have no respect for the group

- You have to earn the audience's attention. You must create a belief in your credentials for talking to them, create a rapport between yourself and the group, make them want to listen and understand – yet perhaps also keep an open mind throughout about what is still to come. Presentation is aided by a healthy amount of empathy on the part of the speaker and you can do a lot worse than think long and hard about any audience you are due to address – the more you know about them the better, and some prior checking is sometimes advisable. If you expect the group to be very different, in age or experience say, from what is in fact the case, there is a strong likelihood that some of what you say to them will fall on stony ground.

32 EVERY AUDIENCE IS DIFFERENT

Points about the audience and preparation are made throughout this book. Here the two are brought together to make one key point that you forget at your peril.

The idea

Remain audience-focused throughout the piece: in preparing you must prepare what suits your audience, and in delivering you must continue to focus on the audience – the particular audience in front of you – during your presentation and fine-tune as you go.

In practice

- Never take your eye off this goal, and remember that it is surprisingly easy to do so; even minor misfits of what you say and how you say it with an audience can jar and add up, producing a cumulative dilution in effectiveness.

- As a dramatic example – the rut it can put you in is a deep one – consider the following example, one quoted in my book *Marketing and Selling Professional Services* (Kogan Page). It concerns a sales pitch for which the firm of architects involved prepared slides to show to the committee of a charity for the blind. They really did not think of the audience – but just blindly (okay, I know) followed the routine of how their presentations were always prepared and based it on a battery of slides and pictures. The absurdity of it only dawned on them minutes before the presentation was due to start, when they found that ten of the twelve-strong committee were blind. The managing director of the firm told me as I prepared a workshop for them: if that can be overlooked, anything can be overlooked. This may seem incredible, but it really is true and provides testimony to the power – and danger – of operating unthinkingly on automatic pilot.

- I remember once agreeing to give a talk about careers in business to a school and finding myself in front of over a hundred sixth formers – all girls. At one point talking about marketing and trying to describe the creativity involved in something like advertising, I quoted a "Sale" sign seen in the window of an outdoor and camping shop in Shakespeare's home town of Stratford upon Avon. It said, both descriptively and cleverly, I thought: "Now is the discount of our winter tents"*. Previous experience with adult audiences suggested that this would make a good point and raise a smile. At the school, however, not a flicker. I do not think a single person in the room (except the teacher) recognized the quotation. Sad perhaps, and I certainly had not anticipated this, but you live and learn.

* *A clever play on Shakespeare's "Now is the winter of our discontent"!*

33 | THE WONDERS OF "B"

ANY SPEAKER MUST hold an audience's attention and this means avoiding any distractions. There are moments when what a presenter is saying is the most important thing and the audience focus should be on them and them alone. It therefore follows that even when slides are an important part of a presentation, they should not dominate.

Yet how often do presenters switch on the projector at the beginning of a presentation and simply leave it on, with a slide on screen, until the end? Do you? Be honest. Think too of how far you get beyond one slide, in terms of topic and talk, before you get to another and bring that up on screen. It is not uncommon for people to talk for ten minutes or more with the slide on the screen behind them having ceased to have anything to do with what is being said.

This leads us to the next idea.

The idea

Only allow a slide to be seen while it is relevant to and fits with what is being said. Do not allow slides to show throughout the duration of a presentation.

How do you do this? It's easy (yet with groups I meet on training courses I am amazed how many people do not know this). You press the B key on the computer. B = Blank. The screen goes dark and will return to exactly the same place in your presentation when you press the same key again.

In practice

- Making this change alone, rather than having a slide on all the time, will improve many a presentation and allow those elements of what you need to say to shine through and be put across to maximum effect. Try it and you will see how it moves the audience's attention. Switch it on and eyes, and attention, go to the screen. Switch it off and they focus on the presenter, for a while at least.

- An alternative, if you really must have something there, is to have a "filler" slide: that's something with few or (preferably) no words but some element of design and color that is relevant but not distracting. Several copies of this can be inserted into a presentation wherever you need a pause in specific visual images so that attention is solely on you.

- So, let us be clear. PowerPoint is a wonderful thing (and perhaps it should be acknowledged here that there are other similar systems). But it can present hazards. If it is ill-used, or simply used without sufficient thought – the automatic pilot approach – it can and will damage a presentation; at worst it can render a presentation ineffective and risk a presenter failing in whatever intention they had in making the presentation. This is included here as an overall point, one to plan for; other aspects of using PowerPoint slides are dealt with in Part Four.

34 TAKING QUESTIONS

THE FIRST THING to be said here is that the decision when to take questions may not be that of the speaker's. If an invitation to speak is issued, then the format of the meeting may well be fixed; this is as likely to be the case both internally within an organization or externally.

Always find out what the format of a particular meeting is, and if you think some variant would be better (either for you or for the meeting), then consider asking whoever is in charge if the format might be adjusted.

Be careful: if you demand your own way in some situations, it may do you no good at all – you may be better to live with, and make the best of, the planned or routine arrangements. Different situations demand different approaches, and sometimes a specific suggestion will be welcomed.

The idea

Consider when and how you will take questions and build in explaining what you will do to your audience. Questions must often be accommodated but this should be done in a way that suits you, the audience and the situation, and which minimizes the danger of a question distracting you and the audience; or leading off on a time consuming tangent that destroys your carefully planned structure.

In practice

Broadly, the options are:

- To take questions at any time throughout the presentation. This should only be done if you are able and willing to keep control as it can prove disruptive, certainly to time keeping. Also you must be sure you are going to cope well with the questions, or an early one that gets you flustered can dent the best of starts.

- Taking questions at the end of the session. This can frustrate the audience and may give you a false sense of security if, while you speak uninterrupted, you believe that everything you are saying is being completely accepted.

- A mix of both, perhaps a main question session at the end, but one or two others encouraged or allowed on the way through. Questions can be prompted at moments when the talk will benefit from some interaction or feedback.

- No questions at any time, though the formal session may be followed by something else that does facilitate questions, for example an informal chat between members of the audience over some form of refreshments afterwards.

35 WITH A SONG IN YOUR…

A COLLEAGUE OF mine was once surprised to attend a company sales conference and find the whole room rising to its feet as the chairman entered and singing the company song (to the tune of "It's a long way to Tipperary"). On another occasion, and another sales conference, I heard loud speakers booming out Harvey Brough (perhaps best known for his group Harvey and the Wallbangers) singing his spirited song "Super Salesman".

So is there ever a place for music at a presentation?

The idea

Use something musical to create a mood or provide a background. This point needs to be here, I think. But I must declare myself to have mixed feelings as I dislike the constant "musak" that assails one wherever you go these days – in shops, in elevators, even in my health club when I am trying to relax, and swim up and down without drowning. Scratch "dislike", I hate it. More seriously, it does pose some problems in the presentational world.

In practice

- Some music comes with other things, as the soundtrack to a promotional video perhaps, and is effective at least as part of the package.

- I believe passionately that there are few sounds so appealing as Stacey Kent's voice and would recommend anyone to listen to her (there you are, if you ever hear of this, I bet you never thought you would get a plug in a business book). But music, any music really, usually appeals only to some people; it may be many or it may be few, and there will always be some that absolutely hate it. So choice is difficult and so much will seem bland or inappropriate.

- Playing it safe, which perhaps includes playing something quietly as people assemble at an event for example, rather defeats the object. If it is not heard, it makes no real point.

- Perhaps there are occasions when something musical really fits and enhances the other inputs, as I have to say Harvey Brough's song did for a group of sales people, in which case take this as a positive idea. However do choose very carefully, and don't worry, even if everyone complains, you might learn something about your taste in music.

36 A LITTLE SUNSHINE

A GREAT MANY judgements are being made as a presenter stands up to speak. Perhaps they are snap judgements and maybe some are rash and prove ill-judged, but they influence an audience's state of mind and thus their receptiveness in the first few minutes of a talk. You want those judgments to be positive; more than that you want to try to influence them so to be. There are various things that you can do to influence this, many of them the subject of other ideas here; ranging from creating rapport, picking your first remarks very carefully and more. More simply, this idea gives you something that is always available to help in those first moments and beyond.

The idea

In a word: smile.

In practice

- Not with a fixed, forced grin, not when it is not appropriate and not when the topic is wholly wrong for it (a funeral address? Although even at that surely people deserve a friendly welcome).

- Otherwise, give your audience a smile. It shows confidence. It begins to establish rapport. It is positive and projects positive feelings. As the musical entertainer Victor Borge said, "A smile is the shortest distance between two people". So too between a presenter and an audience.

37 HELLO TO YOU, AND HELLO TO YOU TOO

AUDIENCES ARE ALL different, of course, and everyone in them is an individual, but sometimes they fall into more than one category in relation to the topic you must address. This poses problems – for instance, do you go into every detail for those who want that or just highlight things for others? Either approach risks alienating some people.

The idea

Divide your audience and address segments of them separately. This avoids the problem stated above and just needs organizing.

In practice

- As you prepare, have the two segments of your audience in mind (it may be more) and highlight where their needs differ.

- Introduce topics as you go through if you plan to focus on addressing one group more than the other. For example, suppose you are talking about something where experience of it differs. You do not want to risk sounding as if you are "teaching your grandmother" by going into great detail for the more experienced people, but must be sure others understand the background and necessary details. When you wish to show that one group is not the prime focus, exclude them, for example saying, "Bear with me for a few moments, I know that some of you are familiar with XX but I must lay out the details for those who are less familiar."

- This tactic allows you to explain what is happening and prevents people assuming – wrongly – that you have misjudged your audience by going into detail.

- Similarly you can "feature" another group in a later part of the presentation to keep everyone feeling that they are at the right presentation.

- The overall balance must be kept, so do not overuse this device, but it can work well and be used a number of times in one session.

TWO IMPORTANT RULES

MANY PRESENTATIONS INVOLVE a degree of interaction. You may want to stimulate some participation, include exercises or just have questions at the end or during the course of the presentation. Whenever anything is done that switches things from just you speaking to a number of people being involved, there is a danger that order begins to fail; timing and smooth running is threatened and thus people may begin to find your carefully arranged logical flow difficult to follow. While you are on your feet, and especially if there is no separate person in the chair, the responsibility for keeping order must lie with you. The buck, as they say, stops with you, but it need not present difficulties.

The idea

Make some rules to keep order; in fact make two. The first states: Only one person should talk at a time. And the second: *You decide who.*

In practice

- Of course the full duties of a chairman go beyond this, but these two rules will deal with most things and keep your session ordered.

- Usually everyone in an audience sees the sense of this. An ordered situation is to their advantage as much as yours; for example it helps ensure good timekeeping which everyone wants. So:

- At a convenient moment, usually near the start (or perhaps just ahead of a question session or debate), spell out these simple rules for your audience and make it clear why they will help them – don't say, "I must insist"... as if you are imposing a restriction.

- Stick to the rules. As soon as you make an exception, for instance letting someone butt in, you show by your example that the rules do not matter and people will quickly ignore them.

- Working this way keeps you on track, keeps the audience attentive and assists timekeeping for everyone. It also allows a fair allocation of time, so that all who want to contribute can and allows you to dispense easily with anything irrelevant.

39   BREAKING THE ICE

TRAINERS USE THE word "ice-breaker" to describe something that at once engages people and prompts thought and participation. It is not only training sessions that can benefit from such a device.

The idea

When appropriate, involve people instantly through some sort of ice-breaker. This can even be done ahead of an introduction of any sort – that can follow at a stage where people have been put more in the mood.

Most often something the audience work together on will suit. For example, on giving a talk about time management (the subject of another book in this series, 100 *Great Time Management Ideas*), I might ask people to compare with someone sitting alongside what they find the worst time-wasting interruption, and usually their answers are things that can easily be linked to the topic.

Or alternatively if appropriate, you can give people a task to be done individually. This can even be set – instructions on screen, perhaps – to keep people busy as the group assembles. Sometimes when I run courses on business writing I show a slide with this task on, just to create the necessary focus on language:

> *As you scan this short paragraph, try to spot what is unusual about it. Half an hour is normal for many to find a solution that is both logical and satisfactory to its originator. I do not say that anything is "wrong" about it, simply that it is unusual. You may want to study its grammatical construction to find a solution, but that is not a basis of its abnormality, nor is its lack*

of any information, logical points or conclusion. If you work in communications you may find that an aid to solving this particular conundrum. It is not about anagrams, synonyms, or antonyms but it is unusual. So, what about it is unusual?

Note: if you want to digress for a moment and think about this, the answer is shown below.

In practice

- Choose something that fits the occasion, the topic and the audience; it may appear odd if it is solely to engage the audience.

- Spell out the rules but keep it very simple: "Take two minutes and discuss with your neighbour…"

- Putting the brief on the screen if you are using slides may help those who failed to listen.

- After the exercise has concluded, thank people and make a clear link with the business in hand as you continue.

The answer to the conundrum is that the text does not contain the letter "e". It is unusual because it's the most commonly occurring letter in the English language.

40 SELECTING THE WORDS YOU USE

YOU CANNOT SPEAK without using words, but what is important here is how your exact choice of words can influence the meaning of the message that you put across albeit perhaps inadvertently. A poor choice of words is easy to make, perhaps compounded by any nerves you may be experiencing, and this is a common cause of presentations not being as effective as they might be. It can even be that one wrong word can switch an audience off or confuse them to a significant degree. The effect is compounded if this is done at a key moment.

Sometimes the problem here is less one of incorrect thinking, and thus selection, than of not thinking at all. In other words, the first word that comes to mind may well not be the best for the circumstances. The audience must be a major factor in your selection; dictating, for example, what degree of technicality may be appropriate, as well as a straightforward level and style of language. The dangers of too much jargon, which would be better explained, is a case in point.

Consider the difference one word can make to meaning and emphasis, for instance in the sentence that follows: The choice of words makes a *real difference to the effect they have on a group.* You can vary the impression given if one of the following words replaced "real": distinct, great, considerable, powerful, pronounced. Which sounds strongest? Think of the different contexts in which you would want different meanings for this: "powerful" to suggest that what is said carries influence; "pronounced" perhaps when the need is greater technical accuracy or precision.

You can apply exactly the same sort of thinking to phrases. For example, continuing the example above: "Improving my presentations skills will make me better able to tackle important parts of my job" has a much more specific meaning than: "Improving my presentations skill will be very helpful". And if what that will do is make you better able to get across your ideas and influence events for the better, then why not say that?

The idea

Use words wisely and think about what you say in this respect consciously.

In practice

- Avoid clichés and meaningless words or phrases ("due to the fact that" – when you mean "because"), and superfluous elements (sentences that begin, "Basically..." for no good reason).

- Avoid words or phrases that someone in the audience will twitch at because they are ungrammatical or wrong in some way. So do not say: "very unique", "about 10.345%", or talk about "future planning" (you can plan the past? This is tautology).

- Experiment with the differences you can make, and your ability to find words and phrases that match the precise nuance you want. This will certainly lead to a more expressive style.

- Word choice can be affected by what one might call "word-fashion". We hear words entering the language or being used in new ways all the time – language and language use is nothing if not dynamic. But words have a life cycle. Use them too early and they are misunderstood or annoy. I still twitch when BBC radio uses the Americanism of "upcoming events"; the more traditional "forthcoming" will suit me a while longer. Use words too late in their life cycle and they are overworked, have lost their power, and may well annoy. Surely a classic example of this is the description "user friendly". Once upon a time it was a neat, new and descriptive phrase; now that every gadget in the visible universe is automatically described as "user friendly", it has lost all power. (I once asked someone in the computer world about the phrase and was told: "User friendly" means something is very complicated but not as complicated as next year's model – sorry, I digress.) Words do change and some eventually fall out of use, so if you use such words it may sound odd and is best avoided. For instance, while some people still listen to the "wireless", most now tune in to the "radio".

- A small, but significant point that is worth noting is that many abbreviations do not sound right verbally. So avoid saying things like "etc." – it may be used in print but lacks any elegance when spoken.

- Ultimately you have to select not simply the right word or phrase, but a well-selected flow of words that continues throughout the presentation. Perhaps more important than anything is clarity of meaning; linked perhaps with description which is pleasing as well as useful in conjuring a picture.

41 SEX... AND OTHER UNMENTIONABLES

THESE DAYS IT is incumbent upon us all to be politically correct. I probably shouldn't use the word "sex" as a heading, though it is fun to have an excuse to do so and besides, books that mention sex sell better than others. More seriously, sexist language, together with inappropriate references to age, religion, ethnic origin and so on, are not just unsuitable, but can get you into serious trouble. Even minor transgressions can make people think of you in the wrong way. And in a presentation any transgression comes across loud and clear.

The idea

Be linguistically careful (without being stupid – political correctness can easily go over the top). What needs to be done is to watch how you use language. Changes need to be made from the past but clarity must always shine through – it is no good being politically careful but misunderstood. Several examples appear below.

In practice

- The he/she conundrum: these days most people avoid an exclusive use of "he" in case that seems to imply men only. Yet using "she" throughout can seem pretentiously contrived, and saying "he or she" repeatedly quickly becomes awkward and tedious, so a mixture of avoidance techniques is perhaps best. Gradually the use of "their" is changing so that saying, "the boss called us into their office" is now usually grammatically acceptable.

- Time and terminology: some words go through an evolution of usage. "Chairman" is the sort of word that these trends largely outlawed, at least for a while; but now, although there is much use of "Chair", many women seem happy to be "Chairman". This sort of thing needs attention.

- Sometimes suggested changes seem to go too far. For example, I was pulled up the other day for talking about "manning the office". You should say, "staffing" someone told me. But surely "staffing the office" means recruiting people to work there, and "manning it" means deciding who is on duty at different times to provide coverage. Change like this seems to me to risk a lack of clarity (and wouldn't doing so be just a little over sensitive?).

- This is an area that changes as you watch and there is certainly some silliness and oversensitivity in evidence, but it is important and deserves some careful consideration; some mistakes are very much to be avoided, and you must usually aim to fit the prevailing norm (which incidentally also usually means no swearing).

42 SOME PUTTING POWER

IN ADDITION TO choosing the right words and phrases, the way in which something is said makes a difference to how it goes across. This is true in a general sense: variety, pace and so on, but also involves various specific techniques that can add to the power of what is said. One such gives us the next idea.

The idea

Exaggerate the devices of everyday speech when you are making a presentation. The idea here is that a manner that might sound too much "over the top" in normal conversation can work well in a more formal situation when you are on your feet. Just as the dramatic pause needs to be sufficiently long to show it for what it is, so the way you speak needs to be tailored to ensure it produces the emphasis you want. This is an area to think about, experiment with and find styles that you are comfortable with and which do the job you want.

In practice

- Two examples of this are shown here (and other ideas also link to this kind of thinking and delivery):

  - Repetition: Repeating a well chosen word or phrase can add emphasis. For some reason, three times seems to work best. Who does not know Winston Churchill's famous wartime speech containing the words: "We will fight them on the beaches?" The "we will fight them" phrase repeats to particularly good effect. This can work well in more mundane circumstances. You can repeat a phrase to focus on the sense of it, you can repeat a phrase to make what is said more memorable, and you can repeat a phrase in a way that builds the confidence that comes across as you speak. Just as the last sentence does. This is not something to overuse, but it is something to consider and use regularly.

- Complexity/clarity relationship: here a final point is thrown into sharp relief by a longer than expected run up to it – *Time is not on our side, it is already October and the year will soon be over, what must be done before Christmas is already daunting, but we can do this. Let me explain why I am sure of that.* The words that are underlined in the last sentence, said more slowly than the run in, and with some emphasis, can be made to make a strong point.

- Usually there are a number of thoughts and phrases during a presentation that need special emphasis. Do not let them fall on stony ground, do not rush them, do not let them get lost amongst a crowd of less significant ones – instead, make them stand out and work hard for you.

TAKE HEED OF THE MOVIES

43

Do you go to the movies? In either film or television you do not have to watch too much to notice that there is one characteristic that marks strong male characters (and probably some female ones too). It indicates a device that can be used effectively in presentations, despite being to some extent counter intuitive.

The idea

Rather than speaking up, there are occasions to drop your voice. Did Clint Eastwood shout the immortal line, "Make my day"? No, he did the reverse and this is what made it powerful and credible.

In practice

- Dropping your voice is a way to achieve emphasis, and this is especially so at the end of a sentence, indeed at the end of making a point. Imagine someone talking through some figures, sales or productivity is up, or down, the details do not matter. As the review finishes the tag line is a link to what comes next, recaps the reason for the review and is an injunction to act. Imagine: "So, at the end of the day these figures are not all doom and gloom, in fact they represent a real opportunity. Let's see what action they suggest." The emphasis here is on the words "they represent a real opportunity" and, while the voice would naturally emphasize this with increased power, it can equally do so by dropping down in tone and volume.

- Try it. Like all such devices you do not want to overdo it, but its occasional use adds to the battery of techniques you can use to create variety, pace and emphasis.

44 PUTTING ACROSS THE MAIN CONTENT

THE MIDDLE IS the main part of the presentation and it is doubtless also the longest. During this stage there is the greatest need for clear organization of the message and for clarity of purpose. Your key aims here should be to:

- Put across the detail of the message

- Maintain attention and interest

- Do so clearly and in a manner appropriate to the audience

Furthermore, if necessary, you may need to seek acceptance and, conversely, avoid any active disagreement.

The idea

Given the length and greater complexity of the middle segment, it is important for it to be well ordered. So resolve to use the simple procedure of taking one point at a time.

In practice

- This needs:

  - A logical sequence: for example, discussing a process in chronological order.

  - The use of main and sub-headings: this is, in part, what is referred to earlier as signposting. For e.g.: "There are three key points here: performance, method and cost. Let's take performance first..." It gives advance warning of what is coming and keeps the whole message from becoming rambling and difficult to follow. Imagine what you *say* rather as a report *looks*: in written form the headings stand out in bold type. The divide between sections of what you say – should be clearly audible. The longer the duration of anything you do, the more important all this is.

45 THAT'S FUNNY, NOT

HUMOR IS MENTIONED in several places in the book, but it deserves one mention here to emphasize avoiding what is inappropriate. This goes hand in hand with something else mentioned in Idea 41.

The idea

Check the use of any humor you propose to use very carefully and like the classic advice given to those "about to be married" – if in doubt, don't (use it).

In practice

- There is a huge difference between weak humor (which may be able to be skated over without too much upset) and something that is, as it were, wrong. Remember that anything seen as inappropriate will stand out like the proverbial sore thumb; it is rather like having a misprint up on a slide in huge letters.

- Jokes, quips and references to personalities (including people in the audience) can easily backfire. Even reposts can turn out awkward; I once heard someone respond to a (albeit rather rude) comment from the audience by starting, "Of course someone of your size would..." They then realized what they were getting into and backtracked. The whole incident soured the way things were going. This example also makes the point that one transgression does not permit another.

- Cartoons can work well on slides (though be careful of copyright) but if something is offensive or inappropriate in any way it can cause awkwardness.

- Cleverness, certainly certain kinds of cleverness, is not automatically funny; I once heard a car company describing themselves as the "torque of the town" – a play on words that has no real purpose and just raised a groan.

THE SOUND OF SILENCE

Of course what you say and how you say it are of prime importance to the success of your presentation, but so too is what you don't say. A good presentation will contain some pauses. The dramatic pause is a well known device, well used by politicians and actors, but many presenters are wary of the pause and a prime symptom of nerves or lack of experience is to speak too quickly and pause hardly at all; even on some occasions forgetting to breathe.

The idea

Slow your pace and learn to pause – the effect on the variety of your verbal presentation and the power it can add to emphasis is worthwhile and useful.

In practice

- You need to get used to how long a pause is or should be. When people dry up it worries them, but often the pause seems much longer to the presenter than to the audience. Try counting to yourself and decide what makes an appropriate pause, then you can do this as you present when a real pause is necessary.

- In a pause that does – inadvertently – get out of hand, divide it in two to render it unnoticeable. Thus if you do fumble trying to think what comes next say something – "There's another point I wanted to make here, ah yes…" – it gives you a moment to think, halves the pause and is hardly evident.

- Try a pause between main points. Round off one point with a powerful statement, give it a few seconds to sink in and then proceed. The combination of a powerful sign off from one point, a pause and a change of tone as you move on contributes to a lively approach.

- Use this with repetition. A dramatic pause is..... A dramatic pause is.... A dramatic pause is... For some things, repeating three times like this works well.

- Let a few moments of silence add positively to your presentations and it will soon become a habit that is easy to apply.

47 | CLEAR AS A BELL

ABOVE ALL, IN any presentation people must understand what you say. Never underestimate the need for care if you are to achieve prompt and clear understanding. Communication can be inherently difficult. You need to make sure that there is a considerable probability of a degree of definite cognition amongst those various different people in the audience. Sorry, let me rephrase that: you need to be sure that everyone will easily understand what you say.

The idea

Work to reliably achieve understanding and recognize that doing so needs conscious attention. There must be no verbosity. Not too much jargon. No convoluted arguments and no awkward turns of phrase. This is as much a question of words as of elements of greater length. Not only must there be no manual excavation devices – you must call a spade a spade – but should you actually speak of spades, they need to be relevant and interesting spades and fit logically in with your topic.

In practice

- These are some examples to illustrate how to go about being clear. There is no magic formula; attention to detail is necessary:

  - Long words can sound pretentious so only say "sesquipedalian" rather than "long word" if there is a very good reason.

  - Certain phrases are not only convoluted, they can be annoying. Among a few that come to mind are: "At this moment in time" when what is meant is "now", or "in the not too distant future" when "soon" would be better. Certainly you must avoid appearing to make things up – struggling to get something clear – as you go along: "Well, I suppose it's like...", "... or rather, I mean..."

- The use of totally unnecessary words: "basically" – at the start of a sentence, or unnecessary, fashionable words like everything currently being "proactive" (what is wrong with "active"?), when for instance it might well be better just to talk about "a response" rather than "a proactive response".

- Inadvertently giving a wrong impression, either by being vague: does "quite nice" applied, say, to a person mean *they are good to know* or is it merely *being polite*? Or by being imprecise: "a continuous process" might just be "continual", for instance, depending on whether it is without interval or never ending. You can doubtless think of more; it is sometimes surprising how loosely language is used. In a formal situation you often do not receive much feedback or know that a false interpretation has been taken on board. You can therefore never think too carefully about exactly how you put things.

- Be careful not to make wrong assumptions about people's level of knowledge, understanding, degree of past experience or existing views for instance, or what you say based on them will not hit home.

- Use visual aids: all (good ones) are a real help in getting the message across. A number of Ideas in the final section of the book address their effective use.

- Include gestures: let your physical manner add emphasis, and inject appropriate feel and variety.

- Make your voice work: in the sense that your tone makes it clear whether you are serious, excited, enthusiastic or any other emotion or emphasis you may wish to bring to bear in this way, as well as watching the mechanics of the voice (speaking at the right volume and pace, for instance).

THE NATURE OF NUMBERS AND NUMBER "BLINDNESS"

NUMBERS CAN CONFUSE or clarify, although perhaps it should be acknowledged that sometimes numbers are thrown around precisely in order to confuse! For example, someone in a meeting might rattle through a mass of disparate costings in the hope that just how expensive a plan is will not be dwelt upon. People often:

- Assume numbers will confuse them and they lack skills in numeracy (finding anything from percentages to break even analysis difficult). Because they switch off to figures, they need to be motivated to appreciate them.

- Have a parochial attitude to figures, for instance they can take in things on the scale of their own bank balance but corporate figures confuse by their sheer size.

- Are overwhelmed by the sheer volume of figures (imagine the profusion of figures spilled out by many a computer program).

The idea

Recognize that many people find numbers difficult to grasp (or need a moment to do so) and make sure you do not confuse, when you should be making any necessary figures clear.

In practice

- The presentation of figures therefore generally needs to be well considered if it is to enhance a message. Some essential principles are to:

  - Select what information is presented, focusing on key information and leaving out anything that is unnecessary. For instance, this can mean that information needs to be tailored – the detailed chart included in a report may be inappropriate to use for other purposes and must be abbreviated to make a clear slide.

  - Separate information, for example into a handout to be studied after the presentation, so that the main message includes only key figures, and the overall flow of the case is maintained while more details can be accessed later if required.

  - Separate too information and the calculations that arrive at it. This can also be done by providing separate backup information.

  - Select the appropriate accuracy as you present figures. Sometimes accuracy helps understanding, or is simply important, while on other occasions it can confuse and ball park figures will suit better.

  - Repeat: repetition helps get any message across, and with numbers natural repetition – for instance, going through them verbally and issuing something in writing or showing a slide as well – can make all the difference.

  - Proof read: numbers must be checked very carefully; remember that one figure wrongly typed, and thus misquoted, might change things radically, and for the worse.

- For example, sales figures may be up but there are a variety of ways to describe this. It might be said that:

  - "Sales are up." No detail might be necessary.

  - "Sales are up about 10%." A broad estimate may be fine.

  - "Sales are up 10.25%." The precise figure may be important but note that it is nonsense to say, as is often heard: "Sales are up about 10.25%" – the word "about" only goes with round figures and estimates or forecasts.

  - "Sales are up about £10,000." The financial numbers may be more important than the percentage (and can be presented with the same different emphasis as just described for percentages). In addition, what the figures refer to must be made clear. For example: "Sales of product X are up 10.25% for the period January – June 2010." Language can, of course, change all such statements – "Sales are up substantially" – maybe, as here, just by adding one word.

  - Present information in a way that makes it easy for people to understand it; for example in graph form.

49 WHEN PEOPLE DON'T AGREE

SOMETIMES PEOPLE DON'T just ask questions, they disagree. They object. This will happen sometimes, either during questions or just as interruptions, so take a positive view of them. After all, people are trying to assess your proposition – weighing it up – and they may well think there are snags. They want you to take any point they raise seriously, and not to reject it out of hand, which will seem unreasonable.

The idea

The first rule here is not to be thrown by objections. In order to do so you must view them in the right way; how this is possible is described below.

In practice

- Regard objections as a sign of interest (after all, why would anyone bother to raise issues about something they had already decided to reject?)

- Anticipate and, perhaps, pre-empt them (especially regularly raised issues)

- Never allow arguments to develop (especially not of the "yes it is – no it's not" – variety)

- Remember that a well-handled objection may enhance your professionalism and thus strengthen your case

- The first response to an objection being voiced should not be a violent denial, but an acknowledgement. This may only be a few words: "That's certainly something we need to consider"; "Fair point, let me show you how we get over that" but is an important preliminary. It acts to:

  - Indicate you believe there is a point to be answered

  - Show you are not going to argue unconstructively

  - Make it clear your response is likely to be considered and serious

  - Give you a moment to think (which you may need!)

  - Clarify what is really meant (if it is not clear what is being said, or why, a question may be a valuable preliminary to answering)

- A well-handled acknowledgement sets up the situation, allowing you to proceed with the other person, and the rest of the audience, paying attention and prepared to listen. But you cannot leave things hanging long; you need to move on to an answer (for details of how see the next idea).

50 COMBATING OBJECTIONS

IDEA 49 DESCRIBED the nature of objections and the need to create the right situation in which to answer them effectively. The ways in which negative factors can be handled are straightforward.

The idea

Answer any objections systematically, in a way that recognizes what will satisfy the objector and keeps the vision of the whole balance in mind. The job is not to remove every single minus from the negative side (there may well be some snags to what you are presenting and this is simply not possible), it is to preserve the overall configuration of the positive balance you have created in the other person's mind.

In practice

- There are only four different options, although all of them may need to be used in concert with stressing, or stressing again, things on the plus side of the balance. Imagine an example where your topic is how to present, the four options are:

  - Remove them: the first option is to remove the objection, to persuade the person that it is not actually a negative factor. Often objections arise out of sheer confusion, for example in talking about presenting if it is said that "I don't have time for a full rehearsal!" – this may be based on an overestimate of how long it will take. Tell them what you have in mind is an hour or so, and not the whole morning they envisaged, and the objection evaporates.

- Reduce them: or you can act to show that although there is a negative element to the case, it is a minor matter: "Getting this presentation right is so important, it will take a moment certainly, but surely an hour or so is worthwhile?"

- Turn them into a plus: here you take what seems like a negative factor and show that it is, in fact, the opposite: "Rehearsal seems elaborate and it will take an hour or so, but we both have to do some individual preparation. Rehearsal will half that time and ensure the presentation goes well."

- Agree: the last option, and one that the facts sometimes make necessary, is to agree that an objection raised is a snag: "You're right, it is time-consuming, but this presentation has to go well and there is no other option."

- Because there are only four options for dealing with the matter, the process is manageable and it should not be difficult to keep in mind during a conversation and decide, as something is raised, how to proceed.

A SIMPLE IDEA

SEVERAL IDEAS ADDRESS not so much techniques of presentation, but rather ways in which any communication can be made effective, and which are especially important when you are on your feet.

The idea

As a thread to a clear, punchy presentation style, remember the benefits of a kiss. What? Keep things simple.

In practice

- To help understanding: remember the mnemonic KISS. This means *Keep It Simple, Speaker* or, as some put it less politely: *Keep It Simple, Stupid.*

- So bear in mind such things as using:

  - Short words

  - Short sentences

  - Short "paragraphs" (sections or chunks between breaths)

  - No more jargon than is appropriate (and explained if necessary)

  - Clarity of explanation

  - Description that paints a picture

  - Signposted intentions

- Group topics/points (groups of three to four work well); think of the way an agenda guides a meeting.

- While "KISS" is a neat way to prompt your thinking, the ideas that flow from it may need some thought as to exactly how they can be made to work.

52 GAINING ACCEPTANCE

THERE IS MORE to be achieved than just putting across the content of your presentation. Here we consider that you may well want people to agree with your ideas.

The idea

If you want to get people's agreement to something, you have to do more than just inform and impress them; you must incorporate some additional techniques into what you do – you must make your message persuasive and credible.

In practice

- Acceptance can be prompted in a number of ways, specifically by:

  - Relating to the specific group: general points and arguments may not be as readily accepted as those carefully tailored to the nature and experience of a specific audience (with some topics, this is best interpreted as describing how things will affect them or what they will do for them).

  - Provide proof: certainly if you want to achieve acceptance, you need to offer something other than your word – as the speaker you may very well be seen as having a vested interest in your own ideas. Thus adding opinion, references or quoting test results from elsewhere and preferably from a respected and/ or comparable source strengthens your case. This is evidenced by our experience in something like buying a car: are you most likely to believe the salesman who says, "This model will do more than fifty miles per gallon," or the one who says, "Tests done by the magazine *What Car?* showed that this model does 52 miles per gallon."? Most of us will be more convinced by the latter.

- It is particularly important not to forget feedback during this important stage:

  - Watch for signs (nodding, fidgeting, whispered conversation, and expressions) as to how your message is going down – try to scan the whole audience (you need in any case to maintain good eye contact around the group).

  - Listen too for signs – a restless audience, for example, actually has its own unmistakable sound.

  - Ask for feedback. There are certainly many presentations where asking questions of the group is perfectly acceptable and it may be expected – even a brief show of hands may assist you.

  - Aim to build in answers to any objections that you may feel will be in the mind of members of the audience, either mentioning the fact: "I know what you are thinking; it can't be done in the time. Well, I believe it can. Let me tell you how..." Or by not making a specific mention, but simply building in information intended to remove fears.

- Even if you build in answers to likely disagreement, some may still surface, so you have always to be ready to expand your proof as you go.

53 AN IDEA THAT'S WHAT?

IF SOMEONE SAYS your partner is "quite nice", you are practically entitled to hit them; if your boss says the plan you laid out in your presentation is "alright", then forget getting approval and if you put forward a "practical suggestion" then you are not doing whatever it is justice.

The idea

Avoid the bland at all costs. Have the courage of your convictions and do justice to what you talk about. Talk things up, not down. Be positive, descriptive and make sure that if you are commending something and saying it is good, then it is clear that it is good and that you do not just say it is, but also spell out what makes it good (and if you are thinking that "good" is rather a bland word then you are right).

In practice

- Watch out! Blandness that acts to dilute effectiveness is a regular trap for the presenter. A bland feeling occurs not so much because you choose the wrong thing to say, but because you are operating on automatic pilot without thought, or at least much thought, for the detail and make no real conscious choice.

- What does it mean to say something is:

  - Quite good (or bad)

  - Rather expensive

- Making very slow progress

- An attractive promotion (as opposed to a profit generating one, perhaps)

- A slight delay (for a moment or a month?)

- Requires some improvement

- A practical approach

All these give only a vague impression. Ask yourself exactly what you want to express, and then choose language that does just that. For example, is a "practical approach" one that is easy to do, quick to do – or both, or something else altogether?

- You too may have favourite words you overuse and which could be replaced by words that are more accurately descriptive. Think about it, check the thesaurus and choose more unusual, precise and, above all, interesting alternatives.

54 ENGAGING WITH THE AUDIENCE

EVERYTHING YOU DO can contribute to the effectiveness of a presentation, and does so at every stage, although the beginning is especially important to get you off to a good start. Certainly the audience begin to judge how things are going early on, so if they:

- Feel it is beginning to be accurately directed at them
- Feel their specific needs are being considered and respected
- Feel the speaker is engaging
- Begin to identify with what is being said

Then you will have them with you and can proceed through the main part of the presentation – and can do so with confidence that a good reaction at the start can be a firm foundation for continuing success.

The idea

The creation of rapport is not subsidiary to gaining interest; it is surely inextricably bound up with it and creating rapport must be addressed as an intention in its own right. So, you need to think of anything you can build in that will foster group feeling.

In practice

Numbers of approaches contribute here. The following provides some examples:

- Be careful of personal pronouns. There are moments to refer to you and others as "we" (and sometimes fewer as "I"). Thus, "We should consider..." may well be better than "You must...." or, "I think you should..."

- Use a (careful) compliment or two: "As experienced people you will..."

- Use words that reinforce your position or competence (not to boast, but to imply you belong to the group): "Like you, I have to travel a great deal. I know the problems it makes with the continuity during an absence..."

- Be enthusiastic, but always genuinely so (this reminds me of the awful American expression that, if you can fake the sincerity, then everything else is easy; not so – back to enthusiasm). Real enthusiasm implies sincerity and both may be needed. Expressing enthusiasm tends to automatically make you more animated, so remember another old saying: enthusiasm is the only good thing that is infectious.

I REALLY MUST APOLOGIZE...

IT ALWAYS AMAZES me how many people either begin their presentation with an apology or include one, or more, within the introduction. There is inevitably something of a negative feel to this, and audiences do not like it. This gives us one of our more simple ideas.

The idea

Do not start with an apology.

Rather, if something might be mentioned this way and must be, then make that mention positive in tone. All sorts of things come into this category. People are sorry that:

- We only have twenty minutes

- It is late in the day

- Everyone is not present

- The meeting was called at short notice

- They have no slides – or so many

It is best either to ignore these, not mentioning them at all, or turn them around, stressing benefits. I like to remember an old saying in this context: Given oranges the job is to make marmalade. You should not be excusing your performance, or blaming the audience but getting on with the job. Do not agree to make a twenty minute presentation if you really cannot do justice to something in the time – if you take it on, it may need explanation but not apology.

In practice

- Accentuate the positive, for example don't say, "I am so sorry that we only have twenty minutes. It's going to be difficult to do justice to this in that time," rather say, "We only have twenty minutes, not long so what I will do is..." some details may have to follow.

- Do not add an apology to a negative just to make it more palatable. Some things are best dealt with factually. For example, do not say, "I am sorry, that question would take me beyond my brief," rather say, "I'll have to leave that one as it takes us beyond our brief" but perhaps add, "do have a word with me later if that helps."

- If an apology really is necessary (rather than a kind of protective reflex) then make it clearly, sincerely and do not labor the point, instead move on promptly to positive matters.

56 CLEAR AND MEMORABLE

A TWENTY MINUTE presentation will contain literally thousands of words and they are not all going to be truly memorable, although they do all need to be clear. There are moments, though, when something special is necessary. This may only be utter clarity: people love it when something they expect to be complicated is unexpectedly crystal clear. Or it may relate to description.

The idea

Be truly descriptive with language and try to make sure that all your description is clear and that some of it at least is memorable.

In practice

- It is worth working at description – stealing appropriate descriptions that you may hear or read elsewhere and perhaps keeping a note of useful phrases. Some examples make the point:

  - You might describe something as, "sort of shiny" or, to put across a specific feeling as, "smooth as silk". If it is the slipperiness of it that must be emphasized then it may need more. I heard someone on the radio recently describe something as, "as slippery as a freshly buttered ice-rink". No one can possibly mistake that degree of slipperiness.

  - Using similes (saying, "It is like ..." as often as you can think of good allusions always helps paint a picture).

- Examples are also important here. It is one thing to say, "This is a change that will be straightforward and cause no problems," perhaps with the group thinking to themselves that if you expect them to believe that, you will be selling them Tower Bridge next. It is quite another to say: "This is a change that will be straightforward and cause no problem" and then link it to something else: "It will be very like when the measurement system changed, there were plenty of fears about exactly what would happen, but the system and the training worked well. I don't think any of us would prefer to go back the old ways now," – though, of course, the example must be appropriate (it would be no good in the example just given if the introduction of a new system in the past was regarded as being a disaster).

57 ON TIME

Permit me to begin with an old joke: *I say, I say, I say what is the secret of perfect comedy?*

I don't know, what is the ... *Timing.*

Sorry, it's an old story; but make no mistake – in virtually all kinds of presentations, timing, in the sense of time-keeping, is important. Like punctuality, something which acts in part as a courtesy and saves wasting time, especially other people's time, good time-keeping shows respect for the group.

The idea

To keep your options open, you may promise little else about what you do during your talk, but make ending on time one promise that is always fulfilled. And this implies the pacing is right and that you do not have to complete the last planned ten minutes in two to do so.

Time-keeping is one of a number of factors that will be taken as indicative of your attitude to things. Managing timing well is a courtesy and a sign of professionalism. At an important function, if you are allocated half an hour, then you sit down after twenty-eight minutes. If you run over time, you immediately lose part of the audience's attention as they think to themselves, *How much longer than the set time is this going to take?* Run wildly over and the audience may run a book on when you will finally stop, especially if they are not finding the proceedings interesting.

In practice

- If you are looking to impress people, then good timekeeping is one sure way to boost the positive impression you give. It is impressive precisely because it is difficult, so it is worth working to achieve.

- So, having established that it is important, how exactly do you keep to time? The following summarizes some things that help (most with links elsewhere):

  - Use your notes to judge time, knowing how long a page in your particular style represents (you also can flag particular points: halfway, at what time you should start to summarize and so on).

  - Rehearse and time what you plan to say, particularly where timing is key; it will help ensure accuracy.

  - Keep an eye on the time (put your watch on the table in front of you to avoid obviously looking at it – you might ask someone else to give you signals but they are not always reliable).

  - Have some options in your material, elements that can be added or dropped to match the time you are in effect taking.

  - Take note of how long your talks take. If you aim towards twenty minutes and run to only fifteen or twenty-five, make a note of why and learn from the experience.

  - Allow for contingency. Think about how much of the time will go on the introduction from the Chair, the coffee break or questions and so on.

  - Remember that the discipline of good time-keeping by the speaker sets an example. It is little use chastising people for returning late after a coffee break, or failing to be ready to start on time, if they know your own attempts at time-keeping are a joke.

- All these are things that may help and – do not despair – it is something that does get easier to judge with practice. While you will not always get it exactly right, if you work at it you will have a reasonable chance of coming close.

58 SOME NIFTY FOOTWORK

Superficially the feet may seem to have little to do with presentation. Not so. Feet, and the stance that goes with them, are both important elements in the way a speaker both feels and thus comes across. That said, here is an idea to help ensure comfort and assist in making a good impression.

The idea

Think about your feet. While it may be true that people in the audience rarely look at a presenter's feet (though you may still want to make sure your shoes are clean), if you make mistakes in the way you stand they will notice both the feet and the results. The first question to be investigated is therefore "to move or not to move". The extremes can both cause problems:

In practice

- Beware of too much movement, this:

  - Can make the speaker appear nervous

  - May channel energy away from more important areas

  - May become a distraction

  - Could put you in the wrong place at the wrong time (out of reach of the projector or your notes)

- Beware also too little movement, it:

- Can make you look uncomfortable

- Can actually be uncomfortable (you get stiff easily)

- Restricts the use of gestures and makes for a static approach

- Circumstances affect cases. You cannot move so much standing behind a lectern as you can do working from behind a table or out in the open, for instance. Always find an "ideal" amount of foot movement that will both suit you and seem appropriate to the audience. As examples of the principle, such an ideal might include how you:

  - Stand up straight (slouching looks slovenly – the best way of avoiding this is to imagine a string attached to the middle of the top of the head pulling straight upwards).

  - Keep your feet just a little apart (shoulder width – to maintain an easy balance).

  - Always move just a little to avoid cramp and add some variety.

  - Move purposively (making it clear, for example, that you are moving to be near equipment or to address a questioner more directly).

- Overall a relaxed, comfortable and yet professional stance will communicate confidence (perhaps even beyond the level that is felt). The most suitable stance may vary depending on both the nature and duration of the event. For example, meetings may be more formal or less formal (a speaker may need to walk into the open space of a U-shaped conference layout to address people more individually), and some are simply longer (a trainer working with a group all day might acceptably lean back, effectively half sitting against the table at the front, whereas a fifteen-minute presentation from a lectern may need greater formality and allow less variety). Stance can make a point too: I once saw a speaker sit cross legged on top of a table and start his speech by saying, "Not all accountants are boring."

- It is even worth mentioning choice of shoes – wear comfortable ones.

59 SOMETHING UNFORESEEN

This implies a difference from an *accident*: these can sometimes be the speaker's fault or the cause is far removed from the group (for instance, a fire alarm rings in a hotel meeting room) as opposed to what is defined here as an incident where others may be involved.

An example will make the point. For instance, imagine that a speaker is proceeding well. Let us say they are presenting a plan to the Board of Directors, when the meeting room door opens and a secretary or assistant enters with a tray of tea. What should the speaker do? Consider:

- Should the speaker continue?

- Will the noise (of cups and saucers being laid out) be a distraction? A serious one?

- With the group being senior (the Board) – would it be impolite to stop or complain?

- Was it organized for it to happen at this time?

- Could it be a mistake, perhaps the meeting should have been left undisturbed?

The idea

There is, I believe, an idea here that provides an important rule: never compete with an interruption. It will always distract and always dilute the effectiveness of what you are doing.

In practice

- The first response to such an incident should be to acknowledge it. The intention must be to:

  - Ensure it is clear you are aware of the problem (someone may well be wondering what the matter is with a speaker who carries on as if no one is distracted when clearly they are).

  - Either minimize or eliminate the interruption.

  - Summon assistance if appropriate.

  - Maintain the overall smooth flow of the presentation as far as possible.

  - Reinforce your perceived capability as a speaker (recovering well even from minor mishaps is often well regarded, especially by those who feel they would not have done so well faced with something similar).

- Consider these issues further by reference to our tea delivery example. This might pose the following options:

  - Simply acknowledging it may remove it ("Perhaps the serving of the tea could wait just a few minutes until we are finished," – whoever is doing the delivery may, hearing this, beat a hasty retreat. In some groups a moment's silence might well have the same effect).

  - Asking the Chair (if there is one) for a view ("Would you like me to pause for a moment while the tea is laid out?" – this may prompt a number of useful responses: from agreement that you should do so, to an instruction that the tea should wait).

  - Adjust your timing so that you can break earlier than planned ("I see the tea is here. Let's break now and I will pick up the point...").

- Remember that it may well be necessary to complete the sentence or the point being made immediately before the interruption. It may also be wise to recap a little if you break and resume later, even if the gap is slight.

- Worth a mention, one regular hazard these days is the ubiquitous mobile phone. A reminder to turn them off is appropriate in many gatherings and the "never compete with an interruption" advice stands: if one rings, wait until it is silenced, perhaps saying something like, "Can't be for me, mine's switched off."

- Some things are so serious that there is little alternative but to stop for a while; for instance if nothing can be heard without the microphone and it goes dead.

60 OOPS!

EVEN WITH THE best will in the world (even assuming adequate preparation), not everything is going to go right every time. Sometimes there will be unexpected accidents and these can throw any speaker off their stride or disrupt the attention of the audience.

Of course, they may do both, bearing in mind that it is mostly fear of the second that causes people to allow the first to occur.

The idea

You may not know exactly what is going to happen but you can accept that realistically something occasionally will, and consider in advance how to best deal with unexpected accidents. Certain things can be planned for pretty specifically. For example, if any projection equipment you may be using fails, how are you going to handle it? The answer may depend on the nature and location of the presentation, but having a few options in mind will make it easier to cope with.

In practice

- First adopt the right attitude:

  - Accept that accidents do, occasionally, happen.

  - Accept that they do disrupt attention and cannot be ignored.

  - Remember that forewarned is forearmed.

- All sorts of things can happen – caused by you or something else. You spill a jug of water or put up the next slide and it is not the next slide. Reactions can vary and include reduced credibility, laughter, distraction, even pity. What is needed is a systematic response, a mode of dealing with things that you drop into almost automatically, matching the specifics of what you do to the circumstances of the moment. The following provides such a basis for action:

1. Acknowledge it (it is no good pretending nothing has happened). This can range from saying, "Oh, dear" to saying something more humorous "Don't expect me to pay for that!" if something is broken, for example.

2. Consider the options, which may range from a further remark or two while you sort something out, to taking an impromptu break while the situation is recovered.

3. Take the chosen action – quickly and quietly and calmly (remember the old saying: *more haste less speed*).

4. Communicate – simply tell people what is happening (this may take no longer than the action itself).

5. Restart with some punch, rather as if starting a new point.

- Remember that the audience are on your side when disaster strikes. The most usual thought to flash through the minds of members of the group is: *Thank goodness it isn't me having to deal with that!* So if something happens that could not have been avoided, then a smooth recovery is impressive and builds the perception of competence you no doubt want to project.

- Something else you can have ready is a supply of "filler" remarks, such as the phrase: "Don't expect me to pay for that!" mentioned earlier. Think about what suits you and store such phrases away: you will inevitably need something like it occasionally.

- Remember, the response to accidents should not be all doom and gloom; they may present a chance to shine.

61 ARE YOU STANDING COMFORTABLY?

BOTH ARMS AND hands give rise to one of the most asked questions from presenters: What do I do with my hands? Awkwardness about what to do with them can be a distraction to the speaker. And if they are awkward then they become a distraction to the audience. They should be an asset to the speaker and make a positive impression on the members of the audience; so too should gestures. Beware:

- Too static a pose is awkward and distracting (and may look too formal or imply nerves).
- Some static positions look protective (implying fear of the audience). This is true of standing with arms folded or clasped in front of the body.
- Too much arm waving seems nervous and is equated with fidgeting (this is especially so of arm waving and hand gestures that do not seem to relate to what is being said – the Magnus Pyke school of presentation).

The idea

Adopt a position and manner that appears natural and comfortable. Doing so can play a part in adding interest, enthusiasm and emphasis, and gives an impression of confidence and thus expertise.

In practice

- The most obvious natural position is simply standing with both hands hanging loosely by the sides. The problem here is that many people find that the more they think about it the harder it is to be natural. The only route is thus to think about it first, to decide on a number of positions that can be adopted as bases from which a period of greater animation can commence, then forget about it. Remember that for men in a business suit, one hand in a pocket may have an appropriate appearance; two never does, it just looks slovenly. One useful alternative to arms by the sides is to give your hands something specific and appropriate to do, for example:

- Hold some suitable item (perhaps a pen).

- Hold onto something (perhaps a corner of a lectern) – one hand is best here, using two can make it look as if you are hanging on for protection, so even with one hand, avoid white knuckles!

- This is certainly an area that can benefit from some thought; however, what works best is a fluid transition between these things. A natural pose, then shifting to another, then making a gesture and moving back again works well. Rest assured it comes with practice and try to avoid becoming hyper-conscious of it. If you relax and forget about it, you will adopt a natural pose and manner; one which will look right.

62

MAKING A GESTURE

You NEED TO adopt a comfortable position and manner while presenting (see Idea 61); more than that, you should be physically as well as verbally animate.

The idea

Go beyond simple movement and animations and make some gestures. Doing so enlivens a presentation and stops you looking too static (and an unmoving position can make you look unprepared, nervous and lacking in confidence – at worst like a startled rabbit in the headlights of an approaching car).

In practice

- Gestures should not be overdone in a way that just looks like random flailing about. They should be useful and relate to the words being spoken. Above all there must be some. To use no animation at all always gives a lacklustre impression. What can you do? Here are some examples:

  - A simple directional pointing – to a slide, a member of the group, or more intangibly (a point into space as you say something about the world at large)

  - A fist banged on the table – 'NO!'

  - A width gesture (like the fisherman's "one that got away" gesture) to indicate size – "enormous potential"

- Counting on the fingers – "First, we need... secondly..." (although be careful not to lose count! – people notice)

- Holding up and showing an item – "This XX will..."

- A dramatic gesture – throwing something (carefully!)

- You can no doubt think of further examples and must search for ones that you find comfortable to use, and that will become a natural part of your approach. It is an idea, at least until confidence builds, to use a mark in your notes to prompt you to make key gestures. Here again we are seeing something that is dependent, at least in part, on acquiring habits. Do not worry about it too much and it will become natural, although knowing what you are aiming at will surely help.

63

USING YOUR VOICE

THE FIRST STEP towards maximizing what can be done with the voice is to be relaxed and project it effectively, something touched on in several other ideas. The voice has an almost infinite capacity to vary meaning and emphasis. Just how something is expressed can add a great deal to its impact. Often even tiny changes in tone can vary meaning. Consider a simple sentence with the emphasis placed on particular words:

- It is your *voice* that makes the difference
- It is *your* voice that makes the difference

Consider too the slight difference that puts a question mark at the end of a sentence:

- You are not sure
- You are not sure?
- And finally: You are *not* sure? (These two factors together)

The idea

Always ensure that your voice has variety – varying pace and pitch – thus producing a suitable emphasis, and simply sounding interesting. A dull monotone will spark no interest and prevent there being an emphasis on anything. Here we review the way in which this occurs and consider ways of achieving what you want from your voice.

In practice

- It is always something of a shock to the system for people to hear their own voices, as when you record something and play it back. Your voice is perhaps a particular shock; no one ever hears themselves as others hear them – not unless they are recorded. Some faults, such as talking too fast (often an effect of nerves), can be quickly corrected once people have heard how they really sound.

- Try recording a minute or two of your voice as a test. If you have not heard yourself recently it may be a shock, but recent exposure to how you actually sound is certainly useful if you feel you want to make any changes to the way you come across.

- Emphasis, in the sense of stressing words and phrases indicated above, is largely just a question of adding a slight exaggeration to the way you would speak less formally.

64 IT'S ALL IN THE BREATHING

ANOTHER SOURCE OF concern to some is their voice, or rather the projection of it. Public speaking should not be a strain. If it is then it will show, the audience will hear the strain and may even read it wrongly, believing you to be uncertain perhaps just when you want to sound authoritative.

Again, this should not be a problem. You may feel your voice is inadequate to the task, but it almost certainly will do the job supremely well. Listen to children in the playground. They all have huge voices, seemingly endless lung capacity and projecting their voice causes them no problem at all. Why should that ability change with age? If it does then it is because the wrong habits build up.

The idea

Don't take your voice for granted. Think about making it work well. The solution is relaxation and breathing. Men and women have voices of different pitch. This means that straining is more clearly audible in a woman whose voice will quickly become squeaky if forced. It may be that some women need to intentionally pitch their voice just a little lower than they would in normal conversation.

The voice is the vehicle for your messages; an attempt to make presentations with no conscious thought of it is akin to setting out on a car journey without checking the petrol gauge.

In practice

- I once asked voice coach and actor, Constance Lamb, for her views. She told me:

  - Most people do not breathe properly when they speak. The breath supports the voice and has plenty of power and energy. If you speak on the 'held' breath, this creates tension and stress in the voice and blocks off the power. You will create the best impact by speaking on the outward breath, by using the diaphragm – the muscle that can best be described as the 'kicker', and which propels the breath and the voice outwards. Only in this way can an actor use their voice to fill a large theatre, and it also helps control nerves. If the technique will cope with that then no presenter should have a great problem.

  - The best way to project is to speak during the exhalation of a breath. Try it. Notice the difference. Proper breathing – in slowly through the mouth, expanding the rib cage front, back and sides (imagine the rib cage is like a bellows) – is the only way to obtain sufficient air when speaking. It fills the lungs fully and easily. And fast. Taking a few slow, deep breaths like this before you start a talk, particularly if you consciously relax the shoulders and chest as you do so, will relax you.

  - With your breathing working well, you can concentrate on using your voice to produce the modulation and the emphasis any formal presentation needs. Certain potential problems can be cured simply by the manner in which you speak. For example, a person who habitually speaks too fast has only to articulate words (and especially consonants) and pronounce the endings of words clearly, and the pace slows automatically.

- It is easy to demonstrate this to yourself. If you receive a shock, you automatically breathe in sharply by contracting the diaphragm, then 'hold' the breath without letting go. Try it. Take a sharp breath. Hold it. You will find that some tension soon starts to creep in. Now breathe out with a big, audible sigh. The diaphragm relaxes and the tension vanishes. Everyday speech often happens on the held breath, and the breath is only released after completing a sentence.

65 CAN YOU HEAR ME AT THE BACK?

FOR THE LESS experienced speaker, judging whether you will be heard clearly at the back of the room is a worry. Clearly if people cannot actually hear you this is the ultimate problem. There is a story told of a speaker pausing to say, Can you hear me okay at the back of the room? They are answered by a voice saying, "Yes, but I'm prepared to swap with someone who can't." Even a situation in which people are hearing only with a struggle can be dangerous, and it will change the audience's view of you. The results of this may include the following:

- The audience tends to become irritated

- Audience attention is less on the message than on struggling to hear

- The speaker may well be regarded as nervous, inconsiderate, inexpert or worse

- A low voice also tends to be monotonous and thus boring.

The idea

Perhaps the most basic idea of all: if you are going to speak to a group, make sure that they can hear you, and do so comfortably.

In practice

- Audibility is in fact largely only a matter of speaking somewhat louder than is usual in conversation. The simplest rule is to direct what you say at the most distant part of the room (keep the people in the back row in mind).

- It is important to get this right – so a test is a good idea, before a presentation in a strange room get someone to stand at the back and see how loudly you must speak to be clear.

- A good clear delivery has advantages; it gives a positive impression of the speaker as someone competent and commanding attention.

- In addition, speaking up tends to be one factor that helps you inject more animation and enthusiasm into a presentation. It encourages you to use gestures and generally affects the professional way in which you come across.

66 | READY, STEADY, GO

THE START YOU make is crucial. A good start gives you confidence and acts to get the audience in an optimistic and receptive mood. You want it to be striking, you want it to jump-start the session and you do not want it to die in a plethora of administrative blather.

The idea

The idea here is simply to start twice, using an initial start to set any (necessary) administrative matters aside and another, different in nature, to jump you into the presentation proper.

In practice

- Tell the audience you will start twice: saying something like, "Let's get the necessary administrative matters out of the way first." These may include timings (including breaks, refreshments etc.), emergency arrangements (like fire alarms), geography, if unfamiliar (such as the location of toilets) – and more. Note: on occasion all this may be done ahead of you by a chairman. If so you may still need a brief first start, perhaps a "Thank you for inviting me" type comment before you move on.

- This can be prefixed by a sentence or two highlighting the more interesting bit to come; otherwise deal with it as a routine but necessary digression.

- Then: pause, make it clear that the "false" start is over and begin again with the "real" start – and do so strongly.

67 THE EYES HAVE IT

To BE THOUGHT effective any speaker needs to establish some rapport with an audience. Much of this comes from how you look, sound, what you say and how you say it. But even then you need to engage the audience in another way.

The idea

Establish and maintain good eye contact with those you address. Doing so makes an important contribution to the overall way in which a speaker is perceived and you need to maximize the impact you make in this respect. Consider first what constitutes good eye contact and which shows the speaker is in touch with the audience. It can give an impression which produces a number of benefits:

- It establishes rapport with the group, which demonstrates that you care about them and increases their belief that the presentation will be right for them.

- This interest in the group increases credibility, trust and attention.

- The speaker appears more confident, more assertive, more professional, more expert (it can enhance any intended feeling of this sort).

- It allows feedback (it is useful to know if people appear attentive, interested, supportive or bored or indifferent).

- Such feedback can be used to fine-tune the detail of what you are doing.

- All positive benefits felt by the speaker act in some way to build confidence and this, in turn, helps improve the way in which you come across.

Overall, two factors are particularly important. Eye contact should be:

- Comprehensive, taking in all of the group (or all parts of a large audience) and continuing throughout the presentation.

- Deliberate and noticeable (this means that eye contact must be maintained for longer than would be normal in ordinary conversation – perhaps for periods of four to five seconds rather than two to three).

Thus it is very much something that can only become truly effective once it becomes a habit, and it is a habit that you must work to acquire (see Idea 77).

In practice

- Read the signs as you do it: do people seem interested, bored or puzzled, for instance (if so you may need to adjust what you are doing).

- Always remember what bad eye contact – looking too long at your notes, away from the group (into the corner of the room or out of the window – *What's so fascinating?* people will ask themselves), or at one or two favoured members of the group to the exclusion of the others – can lead to. It can mean you create little or no rapport with the audience. It can mean:

  • You appear anxious, nervous or, at worst, incompetent.

  • You seem to lack sincerity.

- You lose the level of credibility you seek.

- You obtain little or no feedback.

- The presentation may seem to falter (especially because of any lack of feedback).

- There is no opportunity for feedback to lead to certain kinds of fine-tuning as the talk proceeds. Feedback might indicate incomprehension of some point, which can then be elaborated on (something to watch for particularly with technical points and figures).

- Watch for, and avoid, any automatic pattern developing. It is disconcerting for an audience to see a speaker going through a routine of looking at each section of the group in, say, a regular clockwise circuit.

- Remember too that if you are:

  - Well prepared

  - Familiar with your material

  - Working from clear notes (that do not need lengthy attention to spot what comes next)

  - Comfortable in your environment

  - Relaxed and confident

Then your ability to produce good eye contact will be enhanced.

68 POINTING THE WAY

PEOPLE LIKE KNOWING broadly what they are in for, and appreciate – albeit perhaps subconsciously – help in keeping everything well ordered and in context as you speak; doing this helps carry a group with you.

The idea

Use the technique of signposting (or, as it is sometimes called, labelling) repeatedly throughout the presentation process. It virtually cannot be overdone. It simply involves telling people, in outline or in brief, not only what is coming next but sometimes the purpose or texture of it as well.

It can start with the whole talk. You spell out what is, in effect, an agenda. Thus in talking about a project of some sort, you might say: "Today I want to review three key issues. First, what needs to be done; second, who will do what; and third, the timing involved..." Signposting does not just keep you organized; people like it. They like to have things in context, know clearly how one thing links to another and know – in advance – something about what is coming next.

In practice

- If the presentation is of any length or complexity, then signposting can precede and lead into sub-points: "Now secondly, I said I would discuss the audience; here I want to mention two main, and different, perspectives – what they expect and what they need. First, audience expectations..." Exactly the same sort of process may be relevant down several layers. One point, and something I know I must watch – you need to keep count. I am apt to say, authoritatively: "There are four key issues here, and when I am up to six, someone in the audience will take delight in pointing out that I cannot count (I reply that I *can* count and it is my creativity that is providing the additional key points, but it is still best not to do this).

- Similarly, you can flag or label the exact nature of particular things you say.

  - Specifically: "Now let me give you an example" – an example is coming

  - By implication: "For instance..." – there is probably an example coming

  - With added meaning: "This is an odd way of looking at it but it makes a point..." – an example is probably coming and it is not a routine one; might even be amusing

  - With added content: "Consider this in relation to, for instance, an elephant..." – an example coming up extends the content to a new, and perhaps, unexpected area

  - With an obvious flourish: "You may think that's irrelevant. In fact it's not an elephant, it's a hippopotamus..." – this example is used as a pace-breaking aside with a touch of humor (well, when my children were young we all thought it was funny).

- You can signpost intention in all sorts of ways. For instance, you can prompt people to:

  - Pay particular attention to a complex point

  - Relax

  - Relate what is being said to their experience in some way

- Link what is being said now to an earlier point

- Answer (a perhaps rhetorical) question that you will soon pose

- Signposting can get people thinking along particular lines, adding elements of their own experience to support an argument, or just prompt them to file away one point and turn their mind to consideration of the next.

HERE'S A FUNNY THING

Humor is invaluable for varying the pace, changing the mood, providing an interval and – perhaps more importantly – reinforcing a point. Most talks are improved by a light moment. Some speeches (at a social function, for instance) contain an intentional and significant amount of humor.

The idea

Use some humor by all means, but remember... humor is a funny business and needs sensitive handling. It should not be overdone. It was Noel Coward who said: *Wit ought to be a glorious treat, like caviar; never spread it around like marmalade.* This last sentence is included to illustrate just how humor can work in a presentation. It does not have to make people roll around laughing. Incidentally, quotations are a useful way to inject a lighter touch to your speaking. There are many books of quotations, often arranged by subject, and you can comb the Internet too.

In practice

- Humor can be difficult to judge. What one group may laugh out loud at raises not a murmur from another, and there is nothing so likely to knock your confidence as an out-and-out joke that falls flat. Make people smile inwardly however and it lifts the proceedings and varies the pace, perhaps also having a positive effect on the rapport being established between the speaker and the audience.

- If you want to be sure of raising a serious smile or an outright laugh then it's sensible to be sure the proposed humor is tried and tested, something that you know from past experience works. It is often more important for it to be successful, and pertinent, than for it to be original.

- Short, witty injections, of which quotations are but one example, work better in many circumstances than long stories. If a longer story does not work, or even does not work particularly well, then it can act to dilute the whole effectiveness of what is being done. Because of this, it is usually better to include any humor as an aside rather than as a big production number. If it does not work very well then no matter, you can quickly move on. If it has a moral, then that may make a mark without needing to prove very humorous, and this may still work fine. So think very carefully before you say something like, "This will make you laugh..." How you introduce such an aside needs careful attention in light of the role humor has and how it affects matters.

- The link to the topic is important. Examples in print are not the same as something delivered in the right way "on the day"; however, let me risk an example of the smile rather than belly-laugh variety. Again it is a quotation. The late Isaac Asimov, the well-known and prolific science and science fiction writer (he wrote more than 400 books) was once asked what he would do if he heard he had only six months to live. He thought for a moment, and replied in just two words: *Type faster.* I quote this sometimes when talking about business writing skills and it certainly raises a smile. More important it links well to that topic, showing the power of language, how just two words can say so much about someone, their attitudes to their work, their readers and more. Yet such a small digression does not disrupt the flow, and such a thing can quickly be glossed over if you pick something that works less well than you would like.

- This is not an area on which to overstretch yourself. If the only appropriate story you can think of needs an accurate foreign accent to make it work, omit it if the accent is outside your repertoire. If timing is not your forte or if you can never remember a punch line, avoid anything complex (or tongue tying), or work from an especially clear note.

70 TO, FRO AND BACK AGAIN

SOMETIMES YOU START a presentation standing in front of an audience with a computer loaded with say 20 slides, and you need to speed up to fit the time or move a few slides ahead or back, because you are asked a question. Yet flicking through slides to get to where you want to be can look awkward and members of the audience can feel short changed; they see tantalizing glimpses of slides about which no comment is made.

The idea

Move away from your prescribed order and go straight to particular slides (and back again). This not only allows you to relate accurately to the audience and adjust an original plan as you go, it also makes doing so look seamless and professional.

In practice

- First, how do you do this? Using PowerPoint simply type in the number of the slide you want, click Return and it will appear. In this way you can go forward or back, though of course you need to remember the number you were on at the point of diversion in order to return to it smoothly.

- Make sure that you have a clear guide to slide numbers as part of your notes to allow you to do this easily and promptly.

- The many mechanics of using PowerPoint (and similar systems) are beyond the brief here but it may be worth some study. It is surprising how many people, even those using the system regularly, do not know basic controls such as that just mentioned; hence its inclusion here. It may be worth checking a suitable reference for more details.

71 AND FINALLY, FINALLY, FINALLY...

GOOD TIME-KEEPING IS impressive. Towards the end as you move to finish on time it is especially important. So flagging that the end is in sight may be useful, though you should allude reasonably specifically to what that means. If it is not just two more sentences, say so: "Right, I have two more points to make and then perhaps I may take a couple of minutes to summarize." Or, "With five minutes of my time remaining, I would now like to...." Doing this is just signposting again but if it engenders a feeling, which says something like: *My goodness, they look like finishing right on time*, then that can be good. Good time-keeping may be unexpected but when it is in evidence, it is always seen as a sign of professionalism.

But... there are dangers at this stage and a prime one, curiously, concerns an apparent inability to stop.

The idea

When you say you are going to stop, then stop! Whether you flag the end a minute ahead or five minutes ahead and regardless of whether you are exactly on time or not (though overrunning should be acknowledged) do what you say. If you say "There are two more points I want to make," then make that true. Running on beyond expectations, especially when you have said, "In conclusion..." is distracting and appears unprofessional. Yet the danger is real.

In practice

- The audience can notice an ending that goes less than just right in a disproportionate way, and, at worst, it can spoil the whole thing. So, beware of the following:

  - False endings: there should be one ending (preferably flagged once); if you say, "... and finally..." three or four times then people understandably find it irritating.

  - Wandering: an end that never seems to actually arrive, though the nature of what is being said constantly makes it sound imminent.

  - Second speech: a digression, particularly a lengthy one, may be inappropriate close to the end when the audience are expecting everything to be promptly wrapped up.

  - Repetition: or at least unnecessary repetition (for summary is another matter) is something else that can distract towards the close. Repetition: or at least unnecessary repetition... point made.

  - A rush to the finishing line: the antithesis of the above, this is a danger too when time is pressing. It may be better to say you will overrun by a few minutes, or abbreviate some of your material earlier if time is running away from you, than to find yourself gabbling in the last few minutes as you race to reach the finish on time.

72 A FINAL FLOURISH

YOUR ENDING NEEDS to be made more a bang than a whimper. Summarizing, one of the ending's key roles, is not the easiest thing to do succinctly and accurately. Hence, if it is well done then it can be impressive. Consider this in another context, that of a written report. If, after reading twenty pages, you come to three paragraphs at the end that pull the whole thing neatly together and do so effectively, then you think better of the whole document and its originator. So, when you are speaking (or writing reports, for that matter), this is an element of the whole that is well worth careful preparation.

A pulling together or summary is a logical conclusion; it may link to the action you hope people will take following the presentation or simply present the final point. Whatever it contains, the ending should be comparatively brief.

The idea

Having made your final point – with all the other factors that make for a good presentation continuing to be important throughout this stage – you must resolve to end with something of a flourish (and not with a tailing off "thank you"; see Idea 74).

In practice

- That final word may need to be based on some simple technique (rather like the opening, so only a few examples are given here):

  - A question: maybe repeating an opening question, maybe leaving something hanging in the air, maybe with the intention of prolonging the time people continue to think about the topic and what you have said

- A quotation: particularly the sort that encapsulates a thought briefly

- A story: allowing more time to put across, and emphasize, a concluding point

- An injunction to act: where appropriate: "So, go out and..."

- Having a clear link to what was said at the beginning works well. This may relate to content: "At the start I posed three questions, now let me see what the answers are..." Or it may be just a phrase: "I used the words "impossible task" at the start, but is what we are considering here an impossible task? I have tried to suggest otherwise..." The neatness of such a technique seems to appeal.

- However you finish, remember that your last remarks will linger in the mind a little more than much of what went before them. If you want to make people think, for instance, then your final words will act as a major part of what allows you to succeed in that aim.

73

THE LAST WORD

MOST PRESENTATIONS MAY well be followed by questions; indeed you may wish to prompt them to create discussion or debate, or simply to avoid an embarrassing gap at the end of the session. A common danger of a question session is that it tails away at the end and thus, especially if someone else is in the chair, the final word is taken away from you. What can happen is that, after a few questions, they are slower coming, the last one is somewhat insubstantial perhaps and the chair then ends the meeting abruptly: "Well there seem to be no more questions, let's leave it there and thank our speaker…"

The idea

One important point is relevant here. You will often do best to keep the last word of the whole session for yourself; so organize to do so.

In practice

- If you are in charge, you must keep an eye on the time, accommodating a question session but allowing time for a final word of summary or perhaps an injunction to act (how you finish clearly depends on the sort of presentation it is).

- A useful route for when you must work with a chairman can be to introduce question time in a way that reserves the right of the speaker to have the final word. This can be done specifically through the chair: "Right, Mr Chairman, perhaps we should see if there are any questions. Then perhaps I could reserve two minutes to summarize before we close." In effect you organize the chair into working your way (and seeing it as sensible so to do). Few people taking the chair will take exception to this approach, still less so if everything is going well.

74

NO THANKS

OTHER IDEAS LOOK at how to finish. The last thing(s) you say are more likely than average to stick with people, more likely to need to link to the purpose of the talk and any action that needs to flow from it and must thus be delivered with some real precision. Here is an idea, something to avoid to help make the end what you intend.

The idea

Never make your final words a "Thank you".

It is not that a "thank you" is not appropriate. Indeed, it may well be essential but it nearly always does make a poor last word. What happens is that the talk appears to tail away, a final punchy point being apt to be followed by something like: "Well perhaps I should end with a thank you, it has been a pleasure to be here. I appreciate you giving up some of your time for this… so, many thanks to you all." When this is done it is often not delivered with any precision (a note may list only the word "thanks"); indeed I have heard people ramble on for long minutes.It also distances the words that preceded it from the real end in the audience's perception, making them less memorable and less likely to be effective.

In practice

- The moral here is simple: just resolve not to end with a "thank you".

- If you start with a brief "thank you" in your introduction, this could sometimes negate the necessity to repeat it at or towards the end, or certainly mean that whatever is said later can be briefer, perhaps referring to what was said earlier: "Let me repeat my thanks and conclude..." and you can move swiftly to the real conclusion.

- It is much better, when a "thank you" is necessary, to have it before the final point: "Thank you for being here, I am grateful for your attention. Now, a final word in conclusion..." This enables your final words to be more considered and punchy.

PART 3

AFTER THE PRESENTATION

*"The speaker who does not strike oil
in ten minutes should stop boring."*
Louis Nizer

It is not over when it's over – here we review a number
of things that demand attention after the presentation
has been made.

75 ANYONE HAVE ANYTHING TO SAY?

WITH THE FORMAL presentation complete, there is often time for questions and/or comments. Often this presents no problem; the only difficulty is dealing with them, but sometimes a yawning silence is embarrassing and unwanted. What do you do then?

The idea

Resolve to create – prompt – questions or comment if necessary. You need to take the initiative, but must do so in the right way to make it acceptable and effective.

In practice

- There are several ways of directing questions and prompting comments. You can use:

  - Overhead questions: these are questions put to the group generally, and useful for opening up a subject (if there is no response, then you can move on to the next method) – "Right, what do you think the key issue here is? Anyone?"

  - Overhead and then directed at an individual: this method is useful to make the whole group think before looking for an answer from one person – "Right, what do you think the key issues here are? Anyone? John, what do you think?"

  - Direct to individual: this is useful for obtaining individual responses, and testing for understanding – "John, what do you think...?"

- Non-response/rhetorical questions: this is useful where you want to make a point to one or more persons in the group without concentrating on anyone in particular, or for raising a question you would expect to be in the group's mind and then answering it yourself – "What's the key issue? Well, perhaps it's..."

All these methods represent very controlled discussion: dialogue that goes from speaker to group member to speaker and then to another group member (or more), and finally... back to the speaker.

- In addition, bear in mind two further types of questions, the use of which can help to open up a discussion:

  - Re-directed questions, useful to prompt discussion and involvement in the group and answer questions posed to you: "That's a good point John. What do you think the answer is, Mary?" This makes people think and creates involvement, rather than simply providing an answer by the speaker directed at one individual. Choose people thoughtfully; it may often be appropriate to say why you have selected someone – "With your recent involvement in XX, what do you think, Mary?"

  - Developmental questioning, where you take the answer to a previous question and move it around the audience, building on it and asking further questions – "Having established that, how about...?"

AFTER THE SIGH OF RELIEF

AT THE END of your talk, when you sit down, or later back in your office or home, perhaps with a large, well earned gin and tonic (which incidentally is when you should have it; a drink before speaking "to steady the nerves" is not recommended, and too much may loosen your inhibitions to the point where your tongue takes on a life of its own), what do you want? Doubtless you want the audience to declare it "to have gone well". But what does that mean?

The idea

After a presentation, perhaps every presentation you make, conduct a post mortem. Ask yourself some questions and try to answer them objectively. For example, have people:

- Had their expectations met (perhaps, better still, surpassed)

- Understood everything that was said

- Followed the detail, logic and technicality of any argument you were promoting

- Warmed to you as a speaker (and felt whatever you may have wished to project, for example, trust or belief in your expertise)

- Seen what was done and how it was done as appropriate to them

In practice

- You might want to add to the list above – wanting people to have found the whole thing interesting, stimulating, etc... any adjectives you choose need to reflect your circumstances and intention. Certainly you should personalize the list, maybe even tailoring it to the nature of specific events.

- Asking such questions is just the first stage. Answer them honestly, keep notes of things that went well (to deploy such techniques again) and less well (things to avoid or handle differently) and link them to the preparation of your next talk.

- In this way you can fine-tune your technique, which will evolve into an increasingly workmanlike style over time.

GETTING INTO
THE HABIT

IF YOU CAN remember learning to drive, then the same thing probably applied to that as to some of the tasks of presenting. To begin with, certain aspects of the process seemed virtually impossible – you wondered how you were ever going to change gear, indicate a turn and steer all at the same time – but soon, almost without your realizing it, they became habits and the whole process came together. Thus something such as checking your rear view mirror at certain points as you drive becomes intuitive.

In presenting there are numbers of things that will acquire similar characteristics: eye contact, for example is certainly one of them.

The idea

Recognize that some things you want to do will be awkward initially, but will – often quickly – succumb to this process. They will become easier, they will become habits and you will cease to have difficulty incorporating them into what you do.

In practice

- Do not try to think about everything you want to do at once; it becomes unmanageable. Allow habits to develop, but remain conscious of what you are trying to do – you don't want bad or inappropriate habits to develop because they can be difficult to shake off.

- On the other hand, do think about a manageable number of things and work on them. Eye contact makes a good example: you might vary the way you create your speaker's notes so that you do not have to follow them so slavishly and have more time to look at the audience, or put a note in your notes – a regular reminder that you should engage the audience in this way.

- Once one factor is improving or under control, you can move on to others. Actively working to create good habits makes development more manageable and more certain.

PART 4
USING VISUAL AIDS

"Seeing is believing."
Traditional proverb

There is more to showing a slide than just a click, in fact a variety of visual aids are useful; here are some tips on making them work for your audience.

78 FIRST UP

ONE TYPE OF slide is a regular feature of many presentations. The box shows a very simple example, one that would no doubt feature color and a bit of "design" in real life.

> **MAKING SUCCESSFUL PRESENTATIONS**
> **A review of the process**
> **Conducted by**
> **Patrick Forsyth**
> **Touchstone Training & Consultancy**
> **15 December**

Let us leave comment aside for a moment and jump straight to the idea.

The idea

Avoid using such bland formulaic "title slides": find a different starting point.

What exactly is such a slide, however ubiquitous, for? You need to get off to a good start, you need to set the scene, and audiences like it if you do so. But... this sort of "its-just-like-all-the-introduction-slides-you've-ever-seen" slide is surely not going to be found arresting, interesting, striking or memorable. Just when you want people to be thinking "this seems like it will be good", you switch them off, effectively put them on hold or at least fail to dazzle them.

In practice

- Avoid this sort of slide; people are hardly likely to miss your name as you tell them or are introduced, or fail to grasp even the topic on which you speak (and if they don't remember your name, then a slide shown for a few seconds as you begin is hardly likely to make a difference).

- Find something different, preferably illustrated (see Idea 90).

- If you want people to register not just your name but contact details, the best place for this is probably at the end – scan in your business card to make a slide of it (or pass real ones round the group).

79 THE BLIND LEADING THE BLIND

IT IS A POPULAR misconception that dogs see only in black and white (they do in fact have some limited color vision, and also have much better night vision than a human). It is also believed that color automatically enhances slides. And so it does, but there is a *but*. Color on slides can also distract and can be difficult to see, not because people are color blind (although many are and reds and greens can be particularly difficult to differentiate), but because colors are ill chosen.

The idea

Think carefully when you choose colors. With most people now preparing slides on a computer, and with color being available in profusion at the touch of a button, so to speak, it is easy to pick "what looks nice" when other considerations are more important.

In practice

- Differentiate colors adequately; do not use dark red and brown as the two key contrasting lines on a graph, for instance.

- Do not use white font against a background too pale to allow good visibility.

- Link to particular colors where there is a rationale; for instance to match a corporate color (although you still need to ensure this works).

- Avoid an over-the-top rainbow effect that serves no explanatory purpose.

- Think about the relationship of one slide to others (you may want a theme rather than a plethora of different colors).

- If you want a watchword, it should be: clarity first and color second. Thought of this way your slides will look good, and always clearly visible.

80 WORTH A THOUSAND WORDS

WHATEVER YOUR REASONS for using visual aids (and you may have a particular reason to use them – to help get a large amount of information across more quickly perhaps) – you need to use them in just the right way; being able to do so starts with a clear understanding of their role.

The idea

Recognize that visual aids are used to support your message, not lead or take it over, and use them accordingly. Slides (and other visual aids) serve several roles. These include:

- Focusing attention within the group

- Helping to change pace, add variety and so on

- Giving a literally visual aspect to something

- Acting as signposts to where the presentation has reached

Some, especially slides, also help you keep track, providing reminders over and above your speaker's notes on what comes next.

Be careful. Just because slides exist or are easy to originate does not mean they will be right. You need to start by looking at the message, at what you are trying to do, and see what will help put it across and have an additive effect. They may make a point that is difficult or impossible to describe, in the way a graph might make an instant point which might otherwise be lost in a mass of figures. Think of a simple pie chart divided into two segments to show how much of a presentation comes across to the audience through the visuals, and how much through the person presenting. The presenter's segment should be the larger portion. This is a useful image to keep in mind.

In practice

• The checklist that follows reinforces the point made above and illustrates the general principles necessary to using slides effectively (this is not the complete picture, of course, and slides crop up in a number of other pages):

  • Keep the content simple.

  • Restrict the amount of information and the number of words: use single words, headings, or short statements to give structure; avoid a cluttered, fussy or complicated look; use a running logo (like a main heading or topic on each slide).

  • As is said elsewhere, without a doubt the worst, and commonest, fault in using visual aids is to pack them so full of information as to make them more confusing than illuminating.

  • Use diagrams, graphs and the like where possible rather than too many numbers; and never read figures aloud without visual support.

  • Build in variety within the overall theme, for example, with color or variations of the form of aid used.

  • Emphasize the theme and structure, for example, regularly using a single aid to recap the agenda or objectives.

  • Ensure the content of the visual matches the words you will use (so, for example, do not put the word "logistics" on a slide and then talk only about timing – it leaves people unsure quite where you are).

- Make sure all content is necessary and relevant (a common fault is the use of existing items – a graph or page from a report, perhaps – and then ignoring most of what is there, as you focus on one aspect of it only. People can see the rest, however, and part of their mind is distracted wondering what it is all about).

- Ensure everything is visible. Ask yourself: is it clear? Will it work in the room? Does it suit the equipment? (Colors, and the right sized typeface help here.)

- Ensure the layout emphasizes the meaning you want (and not some minor detail).

- Pick the right aid for the right purpose.

ANYTHING AND EVERYTHING

It PAYS TO adopt an inventive approach; one regarding visual aids as going beyond slides. Practically anything can act as a visual aid, from another person (carefully briefed to play their part) to an exhibit of some sort. In a business presentation, exhibits may be obvious items: products, samples, posters etc. or may be something totally unexpected. Something unexpected, surprising and striking can have considerable impact. For example, there are hotels and conference centres whose proud boast is that access and strength allow you to say: "What we need now is some really heavyweight support," as a baby elephant actually walks across the platform behind you.

The idea

Take the view that the possibilities with visual aids are virtually endless and seek to utilize a variety (perhaps a surprising variety),of things, although everything needs to fit; one is not normally just looking for drama, but to make a point. Like all the skills involved in making presentations, while the basics give you a sound foundation, here is something that can benefit from a little imagination.

Perhaps the most important visual aid is always to hand: it is you, and numbers of factors, such as simple gestures, are dealt with elsewhere. But all sorts of items can be used as visual aids. The task is to review the possibilities and pick wisely and creatively. Some examples to give an indication of how this should be thought about appear on the next page:

In practice

- At my daughter's wedding, a projected montage of photographs of her and her new husband as children acted as a backdrop to the wedding breakfast and speeches, and – making the father of the bride speech – an enormous swatch of paper drawn out as I said, "Now, I understand it's tradition to review the bride's early life..." drew a little apprehension until the exaggeration became clear.

- In a business context I once saw someone who was talking about mining equipment produce a substantial piece of rock: he described it as some of the hardest rock on the planet, then turned it towards the audience and showed as well as described how the equipment he was talking about had cut through it "like a knife through butter" leaving a flat, mirror-smooth surface as testament to the equipment's prowess.

- Items can be produced from a pocket (money); larger things from below the table or behind a lectern (a bottle of wine) or even unveiled rather as at an official ceremony (like a sheet being pulled from over a life-sized cardboard cut-out photograph of a person). Anything like this can work well, and, of course, it works best when it has real relevance and is not just "clever".

82 BEWARE GREMLINS

Is IT ONE of Murphy's Laws? Certainly it is an accurate maxim that if something can go wrong it will; and nowhere is this truer than with electrical and I.T. equipment, and indeed much of the paraphernalia that can accompany a presentation. I regularly see presenters floundering because of some technical glitch (gremlin). A "technical" hitch (and it may not be very technical or complex) can ruin a presentation or at least dilute its effectiveness.

The idea

It pays to be paranoid: check, check and check again.

For example, in the days of overhead projectors (OHPs), the worst that could happen was that the bulb would go and usually this could be easily changed – most machines have two and they could be changed at the touch of a switch. Now what is most often used to show slides is much more complicated and inevitably much more vulnerable.

In practice

- Everything – from the various items that work PowerPoint presentations to which way up 35mm slides are going to be and what electrical leads more sophisticated equipment need to make them work, even whether pens for the flipchart still work – is worth checking.

- Always double-check anything with which you are unfamiliar, especially if, like with a microphone for instance, what you do is going to be significantly dependent on it. And remember that while the sophistication of equipment increases all the time, so too do the number of things that can potentially go wrong. A common glitch is finding that a projector (perhaps that comes with a meeting room) is incompatible with a connecting lead and a laptop brought in from outside.

- The concept of contingency is worth a thought: what do you do if disaster does strike? For instance, some presentations are sufficiently important to make some sort of backup a good idea. Consider printing copies of slides as transparencies that can be shown on an OHP in the event of disaster striking if this would be a sensible insurance (or have a paper handout copy ready).

- Even small things matter. I saw a presentation recently where some benighted gremlin was causing a delay in the system. The click to bring up the next slide did nothing for about four seconds. This was judged no great problem, certainly not one worth delaying the start for, yet after 30 minutes of this it was so, so annoying (and acted as a real distraction).

- Then there is spell checking slides, checking they are visible at the back and that you can be heard and... Enough. If disaster does strike – do not say you were not warned!

83 CAN YOU SEE FROM THE BACK?

IF YOU USE slides, no one is going to pay attention if they cannot see what's on them. Worse, they will be distracted and think of you as unconcerned about your audience, unprepared and simply unprofessional and perhaps not worth listening to. They will have a point too.

The idea

Use a typeface of sufficient size on your slides. Experiment. Check. Decide. Create a rule, indeed consider making it a company-wide rule, and you will never have anyone query this factor again.

In practice

- This often goes with the too-many-words error, of squeezing in all of what it is felt should be said, and worse, reading it out. The typeface simply has to be small and a too-small typeface simply compounds the problem, and makes it likely that people will not be able to read what is shown.

- A sensible type size will act to limit what can be said (see box on the next page which illustrates different typefaces). It is useful to experiment with something similar in PowerPoint, projecting slides in the sort of room you must present in to see what works.

- If you know what you have is suitable for the size of room you are working in, you will never have to ask, "Can you see?" – which, after all, may prompt the thought "Shouldn't they know?"

- On screen in a room (sufficiently large to hold say 30 people), 28 or even 32 point type may need to be the norm, certainly a minimum. With (over)complex slides the problem is made worse and the word element suffers. And note: an apology makes things no better. I have heard presenters put up a slide and say, "I am afraid you won't be able to read this, so let me read it." Oh dear. Worry about legibility, make some resolutions and stick to them.

Can you read this?

(12 point type)

Can you read this?

(14 point type)

What about this?

(16 point type)

Is this better?

(18 point type)

What about this?

(20 point type)

Surely this is clearer?

(24 point type)

Better still?

(28 point type)

84

NOT ON SCREEN

MANY OF THE ideas in this last section are about slides (although there are other forms of visual aid, as is also made clear). Slides were common when 35mm slides were the only show in town, even more common when overhead projectors (OHP) were invented, and truly ubiquitous now that PowerPoint is in common use. This is so much the case that it screens out other possibilities. The habit and mindset of many people is simply: presentation = PowerPoint. But there are dangers.

The idea

Never try to project something that just does not lend itself to projection.

If the wealth of detail, colors, wide format or whatever else may be necessary to make something clear are beyond what can – legibly – be displayed on a screen, and it cannot be reduced to perhaps a series of several slides, then do not use it in this way.

In practice

- In these circumstances, there is nothing wrong with sticking with the "old fashioned" handout: put the necessary information right in front of people when it can only be appreciated up close.

- Handouts can go out before the session (if they will not distract or give away information too soon), or during the session.

- If you hand things out during a session decide how in advance (for example, giving the right number of items to the person at the end of each row to pass along). You do not want the process to take too long.

- Then explain what they have and why, and work through it together, watching for signs that the audience are running inappropriately ahead of you so that everyone remains on the same page.

85

WRITE TIGHT

NEVER FORGET: SLIDES should be clear, simple and any words on them kept to a minimum.

The idea

One way to make sure that slides do not become inappropriately verbose is to "Write tight" – strive to get messages down to a pithy few words. So, if this thought was being put on a slide it might say:

Words on slides should be kept to as few in number as possible, and your writing style must ensure this is so.

But this can easily be reduced to say:

Use as few words as possible and write only the essentials.

But maybe a slide only needs to say:

- Write tight
- Use few words

And perhaps we could lose "Use", or make it one line – "Writing tight = minimizing words & maximizing impact" or settle for "Write tight" alone.

Write tight!

In practice

- Adding something visual (in the above example using a block of text in the background with the archetypal red pen through it, perhaps) can help. There is no sole right way of writing anything of course, but the principle of limiting words on slides is fundamental to making them work.

- A final point about writing, which fits in pretty well here: be careful about spelling and language. For example, this sentence contains an error – its not so important, at least in terms of understanding, but mistakes are often read by an audience as evidence of an unprofessional approach. You spotted the mistake? The word "its" should have been "it's". A small thing maybe, though the incorrect use of apostrophes is something anyone concerned with language will notice. But it's not small on screen. Your every error is up there, perhaps two feet across.

86

BITE-SIZED AND MANAGEABLE

Someone telephoned me recently selling mobile phones. Because such were on my mind (I knew my contract was nearly up) – perhaps rashly – I asked for some details. The flood gates opened and I found myself swept along by a torrent of figures. It was far too much to keep in mind; I was being asked to compare this with that... and that and that and that. I rapidly decided this was not going to be a useful review and discontinued the call.

The problem of getting information across in a way that keeps it manageable is common to presenting. Any mechanism that helps achieve this is worth a moment's thought.

The idea

The idea here is to use what has become known as "chunking". I had not heard the term until recently, so let me explain:

If you want to order additional copies of this book you should telephone 02074218120, but you will not see this number printed like that anywhere else; all telephone numbers are chunked. This one to: (0)20 7421 8120. It is much more difficult to remember – or even read – a string of 11 undifferentiated numbers than 3 sets: one of 3, one of 4, and then one of 4 again. Even in these days of speed dialling, think how many numbers you know in your head. If you want even small children to remember your mobile number (in case they get lost), you break it down still more, perhaps linking it to words or a story.

In practice

- This principle applies to anything that we need to explain, from the chapters in a book – or the 100 Ideas here – to the size of "information units" we use when making a presentation. Any information that goes on and on – losing itself in its own complexities – can usefully be divided into bite-sized chunks.

- This is particularly useful for explaining numbers: telephone numbers, sales figures, projections, forecasts, accounts, etc.

- And it is especially useful for explaining large numbers. As a huge example, there are some seven thousand million, million, million, million atoms in a human body. Unimaginable, but perhaps the sheer size is better explained by saying it is a number 7 – followed by 27 zeros.

- So, whenever an explanation is getting out of hand, stop, think and divide it into logically arranged bite-sized pieces.

87 A GESTURE WITH KNOBS ON

THE NEED FOR variety and pace has been mentioned. Sometimes an extreme version of this is necessary to highlight something and focus on a key aspect of what is being said. Here we review one way of achieving this, one that can add an extra dimension to your presentation.

The idea

You should sometimes usefully add what I call a *flourish*. Such can take various forms. Let me explain with some examples:

- One kind of flourish (difficult to exemplify on the page without hearing it) is simply when at a key point the emphasis and meaning are exactly and very apparently right. Rather as the punch line of a good funny story must be just right, so too a phrase, a summary or key point comes across to perfection. This may involve finding just the right turn of phase, delivering it with just the right emphasis and timing, and with a matching gesture that suits the moment, and carrying it out with apparent natural ease. It is, if you like, a peak of the animation that needs to constantly enliven any address. As such it is an exceptional moment.

  The whole talk cannot be like this, although some need, by their nature, more of this factor than others. Sometimes a particular passage simply lends itself to this and inspiration fires it up as it is delivered. On other occasions the effect is well planned; sometimes too, it combines a little of both. Listen to how politicians speak at something like a party conference as they regularly finish a point with a sentence that says, "Isn't that true, isn't it well put" – applaud now.

- Another kind of flourish involves an appropriate (again usually but not always thought-out) "event" that is added specifically to enliven. For example, I was once in the audience at a meeting where one speaker made a dramatic start: "Ladies and gentlemen," he began, "I know time is short, but in the hour I have available I will..." The chairman, who sat beside him, looked horrified, tugged his sleeve and pointed to his watch. The speaker glanced in his direction for a second, and continued. "Of course, I am so sorry," he continued, "In the half hour I am allocated..." As he said this, he paused, lifted his notes, in the form of A4 sheets, and tore them in half lengthways down the page, thus apparently halving the duration of his talk. He then continued – with every member of the group giving him their complete attention. The feeling in the room said, "This should be good."

- On another occasion I saw someone setting out some changes in policy affecting budgets. There were cutbacks and much carping about certain expenses, now disallowed, although someone had said *it was only a fiver*. He asked if anyone had a five pound note. Someone handed one over. He promptly tore it up, sprinkling the pieces across the table to the clear horror of the volunteer. "But it's only a fiver," he said going on to contrast the attitude of many people towards what they see as "company" money or "my" money. It made a dramatic point (though it cost him a fiver!). I have some valueless South American notes I keep for similar purposes.

- Even so small a thing as a man removing their jacket (suggesting informality or a workshop environment) can inspire confidence. I saw this done once in two stages: first the jacket was slowly removed, and then the braces that doing so revealed. It got a chuckle and made a point.

In practice

- Such actions need an element of creativity but you can plan their inclusion in what you do. There are, of course, dangers here. There is nothing worse than a dramatic gesture that falls flat so you need to progress with some care; I once saw someone fail to make a magic trick work – embarrassing.

The more complicated or dramatic something is the more sure you must be that it will work. The combining of a number of factors, both verbal and physical, to create particular impact is something that adds to the overall impression a speaker makes. When done well, it is seamless. In other words, the whole thing flows smoothly along, there is variety of pace and emphasis and an occasional flourish is reached; smoothly and naturally executed as a high point in the presentation's progress, then the flow continues. The intention is for the emphasis achieved to be more striking than the method of achieving it.

88 SINGLE PURPOSE, RIGHT PURPOSE

SLIDES WITH TOO much on them never do any service to a presentation. The dangers of reading lengthy text are commented on elsewhere, but that is not the only danger and there is one key action, one that can become a habit and seems an easy option, which is very much something to avoid.

The idea

The idea here is never to recycle other things and turn them into slides. Slides should be tailored to suit their purpose and the precise point they are intended to support; most often this means creating a slide (or, sometimes, adapting an existing slide).

In practice

- A good example of the problem is the temptation to reuse something like a page (or part of one) from a report or a brochure and simply recreating it as a slide. It is certainly quick and easy to do, but does it work? Too often the purposes are mismatched: a brochure page is designed to make sense in its own right, to be dwelt on and studied and it can carry a great deal of detail. On a slide this overpowers. The same is true of a report, and here the likely effect is an overpowering quantity of text (along with the danger of being encouraged to read verbatim).

- Slides need to be clear, succinct and almost certainly brief; they deserve originating from scratch.

- Of course, things can be adapted – and abbreviated – although it may still be better to start afresh.

- Overall the danger is that something is turned into a slide and used, despite all it contains, to make just one point. A complex graph taken from a report is a good example. It can confuse and although the one point may be a good one, moving swiftly on and apparently skipping other information can puzzle or cause resentment.

- It only takes a second to click to another slide. There is no more reason why a point should be encompassed on a single slide, than that one area should be written up in a one-page letter, or contained to one page in a report or brochure. A good way of improving an existing presentation is simply to split long slides, which are often long because they were first originated for different purposes, into a greater number (while not overdoing the proportion of slides that are checklists).

89 | PICTURES, PHOTOS AND CARTOONS

ILLUSTRATIONS FOR SLIDES come in various forms and may serve different purposes. Obviously pictures used may vary from a product shot to an example of an advertisement and much more. Digital cameras make some such slides easy to create; downloading a photo you have taken onto your computer and then into your slide package. But if you are to ring the changes and always have something appropriate, you need more than that.

The idea

Seek and record sources of various images that might appropriately enliven your slides, then make sure that you use enough slides that have illustrations.

In practice

- There are many different options here and the trick is partly simply to ring the changes, while being sure that any chosen option suits the point you are trying to make. Consider the following, which you can of course mix and match:

  - Pictures

  - Maps

  - Drawings

  - Cartoons

  - Caricatures

- Silhouettes

- Symbols (£, $, ! and more)

- Note: One caveat – beware of taking any kind of picture from anywhere that might infringe copyright. Doing so could cost you a lot of money.

- Various sources of pictures exist. A convenient one that you can access from your desk is iStockphoto, which you get to via www.stockphoto.com and which is very easy to use. It has an excellent search facility. You put in what you want, specify in what form (they offer audio and video material too) and up pops a selection of photos in thumbnail form. Clicking on a photo shows it in a larger size and you can also check what it costs to download. All the pictures are put in by users – they are royalty free and download cost varies, but you buy credits from the site and everything is priced in that way. So, you might order three pictures and pay 1, 6 and 5 credits each for them. The low financial value of credits make using this system economic. Check it out if you think your presentations could do with some more illustrations.

PICTURE THIS, NOT

SOMETIMES IMAGINATION FAILS, or preparation time runs out. You are left looking at a slide you know is inadequate and seeking desperately for a route to improvement, something that can be done in a moment. One way, judging by slides I see, is at the front of the queue and nine times out of ten it does not help and can make matters worse. So here is another "Don't".

The idea

Do not use or indeed, overuse, Clip Art as a means of slide enhancement.

In practice

* Adding a Clip Art image (or those from other similar systems) can all too easily just turn a tedious, overbearing slide into a tedious, overbearing slide with a dull, standardized little picture on it: illustrated rubbish rather than just rubbish. It utterly fails to address the problem or make a wordy slide work better.

* Of course, less trite, recognisable illustrations can work well. But they must be well chosen, satisfying as illustrations and add something to whatever (words or more) is already on the slide.

As you see!

YOU CANNOT KNOW IT ALL

OF COURSE, CIRCUMSTANCES vary. Sometimes you are required to be knowledgeable, sometimes not so much and on occasion perhaps you must seem – or be – very knowledgeable. For example, I regularly speak about or train on the subject of making presentations. I have to do so in a way that suggests I know a good deal about it and I like to think that I do. But I cannot claim to know everything or pretend that there is never anything that comes up that gives me pause for thought. This is a situation that affects everyone who presents and one that worries some. What to do if you cannot answer something that was raised?

The idea

Accept that the situation described above is fact. You *do not* know everything. You *cannot* know everything and people do not actually expect you to know everything. So accept it and deal with it.

In practice

- First, do your homework. You must not be caught out with something obvious, something a particular audience would rightly expect you to know.

- But that having been done, never be afraid to say, "I don't know". Such a response may need comment:

  - If a question simply takes you (and the audience) beyond your brief or is not relevant, just say so.

- If a partial answer will help a little, give one (perhaps explaining why more detail is impossible).

- If, thinking about it, it is a relevant point and an answer would be useful, say that – you can couple that with a promise to find out and pass on more information later.

- Ask if anyone else in the group can comment usefully.

- If you do come across matters on which you should be able to say more, make a note, do some checking and be ready next time.

92   IT TAKES ALL SORTS

Audiences are not, of course, entirely homogeneous groups. All sorts of people may be present (this affects the intentions of the speaker, as is intimated elsewhere, but it also affects the handling of questions). Different people have different attitudes, motivations and manners, and may put questions in many different ways.

The idea

Be ready to deal with all the main types of people and thus the comments that may arise.

In practice

The following list sets out some examples of types of questioner and some of the tactics suitable to deal with each. Some are all too common, others you will rarely have to deal with, and still others only occur when question sessions slip into more open discussion. So, consider and plan for:

- **The 'show-off'**

    Avoid embarrassing or shutting them off; you may need them later.

    Solution: Toss them a difficult question. Or say, "That's an interesting point. Let's see what the group thinks of it."

- **The 'quick reactor'**

    Can also be valuable later but can keep others out of the discussion.

Solution: Thank them; suggest that others get a chance to speak.

- **The 'heckler'**

  This one argues about every point made.

  Solution: Remain calm. Agree, affirm any good points, but toss bad points to the group for discussion. They will be quickly rejected. Privately try to find out what it is that is bothering such a person, try to elicit their cooperation.

- **The 'rambler'**

  Who talks about everything except the subject under discussion.

  Solution: At a pause in their monologue, thank them, return to and restate relevant points of discussion and go on.

- **The 'mutual enemies'**

  When there is a clash of personalities between members of the audience.

  Solution: Emphasize points of agreement, in a way that minimizes differences. Or frankly ask that personalities be left out of things. Draw attention back to the point being made.

- **The 'pig-headed'**

  A person who absolutely refuses, perhaps through prejudice, to accept points that are being discussed.

  Solution: Throw their points to the group; have them straighten the person out. Mention that time is short and that you will be glad to discuss it with them later.

- **The 'digresser'**

  Who takes the discussion too far off track.

  Solution: Take the blame yourself. Say, "Something I said must have led you off the subject; this is what we should be discussing..."

- **The 'professional gripe'**

  Who makes overtly political points.

  Solution: Politely point out that the group cannot change policy here; the objective is to operate as best as it can under the present system. Or better still, have a member of the group answer him.

- **'The 'whisperers'**

  Who hold private conversations, which while they could be related to the subject, are distracting.

  Solution: Do not embarrass them. Direct some point to one of them by name; ask an easy question. Or repeat the last point and ask for comments. Get them away from their separate conversation.

- **The 'inarticulate'**

  Who has ideas but cannot put them across.

  Solution: Say, "Let me repeat that..." (then put it in clearer language)

- **The 'mistaken'**

  Who is clearly wrong.

  Solution: Say, "That's one way of looking at it, but how can we reconcile that with... (state the correct point)?"

- **The 'silent'**

    Who could be shy, bored, indifferent, insecure, or who just might be taking things in and listening carefully.

    Solution: Depends on what is causing their silence. If the person is bored or indifferent, try asking a provocative question, one you think they might be interested in. If shy, compliment them when they do say something, and then ask them direct questions from time to time to draw them in.

DRAW THEM
A DIAGRAM

IT IS SAID that a picture is worth a thousand words, and pictures have their place, but in business, diagrams are probably more useful.

The idea

Illustrate some of your points with a diagram and lead people through it, explaining as you go.

In practice

- With diagrams the greatest danger is confusing by presenting too much information, or too much at once or on one slide. Colors are important to many diagrams and must be selected to differentiate clearly between different elements. Keep diagrams simple and prevent people from:

  - Missing the message because it is buried in a mass of information, much of which is either irrelevant or not referred to for some reason.

  - Resenting the fact that they appear to be missing something: "Wait a minute, what was all that?"

If a lot of information is essential, it may be necessary to spread it across a number of slides or handle matters another way, perhaps with a handout that can be studied in detail.

- One specialized form of diagram is the graph: these work well on slides, especially simple ones like pie charts and bar charts;

everything mentioned here about clarity is important on slides, they paint a powerful picture but only if they are clear.

- You might:

  - Add different elements progressively as your explanation unfolds

  - Watch for any numbers that identify what is going on; especially on graphs, they must be legible

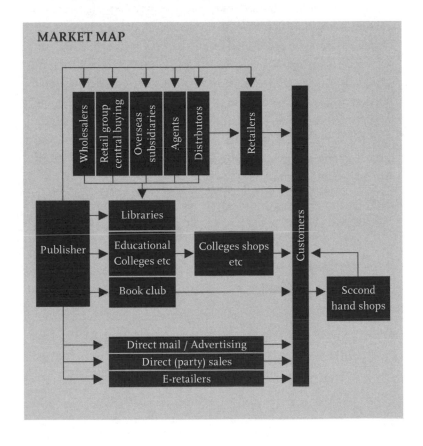

A detailed example must be about something, and the concept here is ultimately straightforward. A market map illustrates the channels involved in marketing a particular product, in this case books. Such a map is not just a device to explain the complexity of the various chains of distribution that exist in every industry (and which are more complex in some than others). It is designed to remind marketing people that distribution is a marketing variable: that is an organization can decide which channels to work through, which to major on and perhaps which to leave on the sidelines or ignore. Such decisions must be predicated on the basis of fact, so an analysis of what proportion of business is flowing through the different channels is necessary – hence adding in sales figures can extend the usefulness of the map. Many of the ways in which products and services are made available result from this sort of analysis and the market map provides a very useful device in planning and implementing marketing strategies. All this comes from one powerful diagram.

NOTE: this example and chart is adapted from my book *"Marketing: A guide to the fundamentals (The Economist)*

CRUCIAL MODERN TECHNOLOGY

THE TRUSTY OVERHEAD projector (OHP) has largely been superseded now but as those (like me) brought up on its use moved to PowerPoint, many found habits hard to change. It is easier, for instance, to change the running order with a pile of OHP slides in front of you. If you want or need to fine-tune as you go, then you just slip out a slide originally destined for later showing and the audience may well not even be aware of the difference. Changes on PowerPoint require a pause and then, unless you stand to block the screen, the audience see your (perhaps fumbling) attempts to make a change. There are other differences too, but technology moves on and one at least of the major weaknesses of PowerPoint can now be overcome.

The idea

Use PowerPoint as you would a flipchart or an overhead projector with an additional acetate placed over the slide being shown – and highlight things as you go.

In practice

- Of course, slides can have pre-planned emphasis built in. You can build up a single slide, changing things progressively or adding elements to it at the touch of a button and this can be very effective (provided the emphasis is well-chosen).

- Now you can do the same on an unplanned basis as you go using just a pen. Well strictly not just a pen, rather a digital pen. Alhough this will doubtless change, the device of the moment as this is written is the Oxford Papershow digital pen. With this neat and economic device you get a kit: you plug a little device the size of a memory stick into your computer, and write with the pen on a pad – and what you write appears on the slide being shown. You can literally produce a new slide or enhance something, ringing a word in red, underlining or adding words. As you do this you can choose the color and the thickness of the line that will appear. It works in a variety of other ways too, for instance you can save slide shows on the "stick" – worth checking out.

- Not only does this allow fine-tuning, additions and emphasis, its use enhances professionalism; people always like it if a presenter gives evidence of adjusting to circumstances rather than just giving a totally pre-planned performance, however good.

95

WHEN TO PICTURE WHAT

THIS POINT DESERVES a place of its own, but stems from thoughts about how exactly to prepare (see Idea 14). A systematic approach to preparation is advocated, and certainly the modern reflex of having a presentation to do and clicking the computer into PowerPoint is not the best way. So what about slides: when do you prepare those?

The idea

Prepare slides in the context of the whole presentation, remembering that they should be designed to support the presentation and not take over or lead; therefore logically their preparation should not lead either.

In practice

- Let's look back at the stages of preparation recommended in Idea 14 again (indeed you might want to look at the two together):

  - List: it is probably best to ignore slides here completely and concentrate on reviewing content and points to be covered.

  - Sort: here, especially if you are a regular slide user, it will be difficult to ignore them completely. It may be useful to add to your note (just a letter S – S1, S2 etc. – perhaps in a color to make it stand out) of where you see slides going. You may even identify slides you have on file that you want to use, but it is not necessary, or perhaps desirable, to identify all the places where a slide will be deployed at this point and certainly not how they will look in detail.

- Arrange: as you get more organized the notes you make about slides may increase; you do not, after all, want to fail to note an idea that crosses your mind.

- Review: slides can be subject to a quick review here along with everything else.

- Prepare the message: here content and illustration go hand in hand. You might still leave exactly how a slide will look for later in order to keep the thread of your overall message intact. If so, then a last run through will add final details about the slides and complete the message. Essentially, slide preparation may therefore go in two stages. First, you decide where in the content a point needs a slide to back it up or assist your verbal explanation. Secondly, you need the detail of how it will do this and what element of visualization it might include.

96 MULTIPURPOSE, MINIMAL EFFECTIVENESS

SLIDES ARE OFTEN considered and used on automatic pilot; they are simply a given. If we have to make a presentation we log into PowerPoint and make some slides. Fair enough, probably the majority of presentations need some visual aids in whatever form. Despite their familiarity, slides and their purpose stand some analysis.

The idea

Make slides fit for their prime purpose and never forget: slides are first and foremost used to provide guidance for the audience.

In practice

- Remember that slides are often regarded as having three disparate purposes. Presenters regard them as being:

  - What the audience sees

  - A prompt for themselves as to what to say next (speaker's notes should do this)

  - A handout to be given to people afterwards as a resume note (this role can be extended if, for some reason, they are regarded as also providing hard copy for people who have not heard the presentation)

- The danger is clear. In part because slides are so often the first thing that is prepared (which is maybe not best, see Idea 95), they end up trying to do all these different things and being less than ideally suited for any one of them. At worst they become primarily designed to help the presenter and the needs of the audience are sidelined.

- In preparing slides, their prime purpose – that of guiding the audience – must be the paramount consideration. If they are adapted to fulfil other roles later that is fine, and besides there is no reason why there cannot be two or three different versions of a slide. For example, this might mean that a slide is embedded in a longer document to create a handout, a document that includes additional information. Or it might mean changes being made to certain slides in the handout version, extending their content to make them more explanatory on their own away from what was said when they were seen on screen. This concept may mean a little more time is taken in preparation, but it need not be too much and is a small price to pay for getting everything right.

97 WITH A LITTLE HELP FROM YOUR FRIENDS

PowerPoint can do extraordinary things. Buried in that seeming simple piece of software is a resource that can produce visuals that are unbelievably striking: full of color, movement and images and which truly deserve the term "visual aid". There are bells and whistles here in abundance, including the ability to add movie footage and sound – dialogue, music, sound effects and more. These things may be possible, but it can be time consuming and sometimes expensive to prepare such slides – hence the next idea.

The idea

Get someone else to prepare slides for you. Provided you give a clear brief this can be very effective, although I would add a note of caution to anyone seeking to get a complete talk written for them as well; having a complete text makes it difficult to resist reading it verbatim and the dangers of that are mentioned elsewhere. Certainly sub-contraction (which could be internal or external) can make using more sophisticated slides more possible.

In practice

- The full potential of really sophisticated slides is somewhat beyond our brief here but if you are interested, check out the book *Killer Presentations*, which I wrote with Nick Oulton, and is published by How-to-Books. His organization, m62 Visual Communications, is a leader in this field, so much so that it has been described thus by the vice president of IT giant Symantec:

"These guys know more about PowerPoint than anybody else on the face of the planet". Its focus is on marketing presentations, and the sales pitches involved in big ticket selling, but the description and illustrations of what can be done with PowerPoint simply amazes many people.

- *Killer Presentations* also provides links to Nick's website so readers can see a moving presentation as they read about it. For anyone wanting to see examples of just what is possible, this site is well worth a look (www.m62.net) and is recommended to readers as it will help you visualize the effects of color and movement hinted at here. I have seen Nick present a number of times and am still surprised by what is possible when I see his slides.

- Realistically (except for certain applications), the time and cost of preparing such sophisticated slides is beyond most people, hence the idea of sub-contraction. For a step in the direction of greater sophistication, I have written separately about the pitfalls and opportunities of using PowerPoint in *The PowerPoint Detox* (Kogan Page).

98 SHAPING UP FOR SUCCESS

WHILE YOU MAY categorize everything you say in a presentation as pearls of wisdom, there will doubtless be certain things that you particularly want people to remember. To achieve this you emphasize them, you may even label them – "Don't forget this!" – and they probably warrant a slide as part of that emphasis. Other Ideas deal with enlivening and making a slide more memorable by using pictures, cartoons or diagrams. But not everything lends itself to a picture or diagram (quite apart from the time taken to prepare more complex slides), so what do you do then, when all you have is a checklist of words?

The idea

Arrange checklists into shapes to link to how the mind works and this can provide an additional trigger to memory.

In practice

- If there are, say, four or five points to remember, people find them easier to call to mind when they first remember that there were say four. They list them off, saying to themselves, "Four points: one, two, three – one more, what was it? Four."

- At its simplest this can be graphically very straightforward: four points might be shown against a plus sign, five arranged around a star and so on, and basic shapes retained and used again

- If time and import allow, then the graphics can be made more sophisticated but as a memory aid, the shape is the important thing psychologically and that should be clear and stark.

- Incidentally, while there is not an easy shape for say nine key points (this might in any case be too many to crowd onto one slide); split them onto two slides and they will also become more manageable.

99 SEEING IS BELIEVING

PRACTICE MAKES PERFECT and there is no doubt that experience can, carefully utilized, improve presentational style and performance. Whatever aptitude you have for presenting and however much you bone up on the techniques, there is one thing that can provide accelerated experience and can do so either formally or informally.

The idea

See or hear a recording of your presenting. Whether you do this or get help to do it, actually seeing and hearing how you come across – warts and all – is invaluable, if apt to be a little uncomfortable.

In practice

- Ideally a video recording is best but a sound recording is easier (it can be done in your office or at home) and it certainly helps to hear how you sound – and yes, that is how you sound, no one hears their voice as others hear it.

- This can be done in a training environment. Certainly I, like most training consultants, recommend the use of practice, recording and critique as part of training in this area and can vouch for the difference it can make.

- It can also be done informally. Video cameras are common enough these days and no elaborate facilities are necessary. You can also link this to informal critique with colleagues (although, forgive the plug, a trainer will have experience of how faults can be removed, which is what really matters).

- However it is done, it can be a valuable part of the fine-tuning that is necessary if your presentations are to continue to achieve what you want.

100 A FINAL IDEA

As a LAST point (well, before the Afterword), here is an idea that will speed up the preparation of future presentations and link one to another.

The idea

Always store your slide presentations safely. What you have done in the past may save you time in preparing new presentations. Storage of slides is usually going to be on a computer, so all the usual rules about backup apply.

In practice

- Make sure you have everything necessary stored safely: slides on computer, perhaps a paper copy and any other speaker's notes or references (including details like duration).

- Safely stored means labelled in a systematic and clear way. I must confess I have computer files marked only with a presentation date, or using a phrase like "Onwards & Upwards presentation: Singapore" without even a date. What? As I talk regularly on the subject involved – career management* – this is not, I confess, very clever.

  That said, note the following: although a past presentation may be a good starting point in preparing another one and working that way saves time, doing so is not a panacea – each presentation needs to be individually tailored to its audience and purpose. So be sure to make sufficient change and remember that sometimes it is better to start with a clean sheet of paper and leave what you have done in the past on one side.

* Career management is a subject I have covered in the book *Detox your career* (also published by Marshall Cavendish)

AFTERWORD

The golden rule for all presenters is to imagine that you are in the audience.

David Martin

If you are to be effective at presenting, there are essentially two aspects to what must be done to create, maintain and enhance your speaking skills. The first, assisted I hope by reading this book, is to have a sound appreciation of the techniques and processes that make a presentation go well; discussions with colleagues, training films, rehearsal and review all help. Knowledge of what works well provides the foundation from which you can work and expand your capabilities. Secondly, you need practice. This can come from attending a course and, if that involves using video (recording what participants do) not only do you have a chance to see how you come across, you could also discuss the detail of this with other group members and the tutor. A course will also allow you quickly to see other examples of the kinds of things that have to be tackled in a variety of different presentational situations. Or, of course, you can gain experience from actually making real presentations, and the idea of actively seeking out opportunities to accelerate that experience has been mentioned in the text.

Presentation is a skill where the process of adding usefully to your experience is, you will find, never-ending. This means there is certainly opportunity to extend learning and practice, and make no mistake, no matter what you may have already done, presentational skill cannot have too much practice, providing that you remain objective and are prepared to analyze honestly what you do (and take on board any feedback from others). Then you can ensure your techniques will improve continually.

The rewards in corporate and career terms, and in a social context too, of developing good presentational skills are considerable. What is more, good habits do set in, a process that is more likely if you set out to make it so. If you develop the habit of preparing, for example, and develop good habits regarding exactly how you go about it, then you will find your whole approach will act to help the end result. A good system for preparing your notes will prompt you to ask yourself if there should be a visual aid at certain points, and whether there are sufficient of them overall, and to do this more certainly and effectively. Good and sufficient visual aids will, in turn, augment the presentation. The thinking and the process create a positive loop. Moreover, practice will soon begin to take some of the chore out of the whole process. Preparation does not take as long for those who know how to go about it and who have a good system for doing it, for example. Even seemingly awkward factors, such as judging how long a message will take to run through, become more certain with practice.

Beyond all this, to a degree, the sky is the limit. The best presenters make it look very easy, although this may simply disguise careful preparation, rehearsal and execution. Training, study, practice and sensible consideration of how you have done can help everyone move towards an acceptable standard. But it can do more than this. Charisma, often regarded (indeed defined) as a gift, actually consists (certainly in part) of intentionally applied techniques. Good eye contact, appropriate verbal emphasis, a careful choice of words and gestures, the confidence to hold a pause – and more – all add cumulatively to the charisma rating someone may be regarded as projecting. But such techniques can all be learned, developed and deployed to enhance the overall effect. This is not to say that such a process is contrived. Something like genuine enthusiasm is infectious. For the rest, in many ways it adds up to a respect for the audience and the occasion. The last thing people want is to sit through a lacklustre presentation. Those who work at how they do it, use the available techniques appropriately and let their personality contribute make the best job of it, helping both the audience and themselves. The alternative, a dreary presentation and an audience who resent it, is not a happy one.

I hope you will find that the content of this book will act as a catalyst, giving you some ideas both to implement and deploy immediately, and others to work on and adapt. The rest is up to you. You are the only coach who is always there when you get up to speak. If you have already had some practice, considering what you are doing against the knowledge of ideas set out here will help you seek to achieve an even higher standard. If you are nervously awaiting your first outing: go for it. You will now know something of the techniques involved and how they can assist to give you confidence. Whatever stage you may be at, aim to surprise yourself and your audience; you may just find that not only does it go well, but that you enjoy doing it. Certainly there is considerable satisfaction to be had from a presentation well made.